D1175822

Provinces
and
Provincial Capitals
of the World

Second Edition

compiled by
Morris Fisher

The Scarecrow Press, Inc.
Metuchen, N.J., & London 1985

Library of Congress Cataloging in Publication Data

Fisher, Morris.
   Provinces and provincial capitals of the world.

   Includes index.
   1. Gazetteers. 2. Administrative and political
division—Dictionaries. 3. Capitals (Cities)—Dictionaries. I. Title.
G103.5.F57 1985   910'.3'21   83–22125
ISBN 0–8108–1758–6

Contents

Introductory Notes

For purposes of local administration, each country of the world divides its own particular geographical area into specific units of local government. The designations of these primary or "first-level" units vary greatly from nation to nation. In some countries they are called "states" or "provinces." Other countries use designations such as "territories," "republics," "regions," "counties," "parishes," "autonomous areas," "departments," "districts," "municipalities," and "divisions," to name just a few. This compilation presents information on these so-called major administrative units, leaving to other sources details on the minor or second- and third-level governmental subdivisions.

In order to make this compilation as inclusive as possible, no attempt has been made to confer legitimacy on or to distinguish in any manner between "independent," "quasi-independent," or "dependent" countries and territories. The only requisite for its selection lies in the fact that, at the time of publication, it was generally recognized as a distinct area with some sort of population and with some sort of governmental control.

For each of the 224 countries in this current compilation, each country is listed with the following specific seven-item arrangement:

(1)   the commonly used name of the country
(2)   the official name of the country in its accepted English form
(3)   the official name of the country in its Romanized native form
(4)   the general location of the country
(5)   the capital of the country
(6)   the number of, and type of, major administrative units or provinces into which the country is divided either for purposes of regional government or of statistical data
(7)   the naming of each of these administrative units along with their respective capitals

(1) AFGHANISTAN

(2) The Democratic Republic of Afghanistan

(3) Doulat I Jumhouri ye Afghánistán

(4) Afghanistan is an inland country of Asia, bounded on the east
     and south by Pakistan, on the north and northeast by the
     U.S.S.R. and China, and on the west by Iran.

(5) Kabul

(6) Afghanistan comprises 26 administrative units known as prov-
     inces

Provinces	Capitals
1. Herat	Herat
2. Farah	Farah
3. Nimruz	Zaranj
4. Helmand	Bust
5. Qandahar	Qandahar
6. Zabul	Kalat-i-Ghilzai
7. Ghazi	Ghazi
8. Paktia	Gardez
9. Logar	Baraki
10. Kabul	**Charikar**
11. Nangarhar	Jalal-Kut
12. Laghman	Faizabad
13. Takhar	Taliqan
14. Kunduz	Kunduz
15. Samangan	Samangan
16. Balkh	Mazar-i-Sharif
17. Jozjan	Shibarkhan
18. Fariab	Maimana
19. Badghis	Qala-i-Naw
20. Ghor	Daulat Yar
21. Bamian	Bamian
22. Uruzghan	Tarin-Kut
23. Maydan	Maydan
24. Parwan	Mahmud-Ragi
25. Badakhsan	Faizabad
26. Baghlan	Baghlan

1

(1) ALBANIA

(2) The People's Socialist Republic of Albania

(3) Republíka Popullóre Socialiste e Shqipërísë

(4) Albania is bordered by Yugoslavia to the north and east, Greece to the south, and the Adriatic and Ionian Seas to the west.

(5) Tirana

(6) Albania comprises 27 administrative units; 1 Independent City called Tirana, and 26 Districts or "rrethe."

Rrethe	Capitals
1. Berat	Berat
2. Dibrë	Dibrë
3. Durrës	Durrës
4. Elbasan	Elbasan
5. Fier	Fier
6. Gramsh	Gramsh
7. Gjirokastër	Gjirokastër
8. Kolonjë	Kolonjë
9. Korcë	Korcë
10. Krujë	Krujë
11. Kukës	Kukës
12. Lezhë	Lezhë
13. Librazhd	Librazhd
14. Lushnjë	Lushnjë
15. Mat	Burrel
16. Mirditë	Rrëshen
17. Përmet	Përmet
18. Pogradec	Pogradec
19. Pukë	Pukë
20. Sarandë	Sarandë
21. Skrapar	Çorovodë
22. Shkodër	Shkodër
23. Tepelenë	Tepelenë
24. Tirana	Tirana
25. Tropojë	Bajram Curri
26. Vlorë	Vlorë

(1) ALGERIA

(2) Algerian Democratic People's Republic

2

(3) El Djemhouria El Dzazaïria Eddemokratia Echaabia

(4) Algeria is situated between Morocco and Tunisia. It is the largest of the three countries in northwestern Africa comprising the "Maghreb" area.

(5) Algiers

(6) Algeria comprises 31 administrative units known as Governorates or "Willayaat."

Willayaat	Capitals
1. Adrar	Adrar
2. Alger	Alger
3. Annaba	Annaba
4. Batna	Batna
5. Bechar	Bechar
6. Bejaia	Bejaia
7. Biskra	Biskra
8. Blida	Blida
9. Bouira	Bouira
10. Constantine	Constantine
11. Djelfa	Djelfa
12. El Asnam	El Asnam
13. Guelma	Guelma
14. Jijel	Jijel
15. Laghouat	Laghouat
16. Mascara	Mascara
17. Médéa	Médéa
18. Mostaganem	Mostaganem
19. **Ouahran**	Ouahran
20. Ouargla	Ouargla
21. Oum Bouaghi	Oum Bouaghi
22. Saida	Saida
23. Sétif	Sétif
24. Sidi-Bel-Abbès	Sidi-Bel-Abbès
25. Skikda	Skikda
26. Tamanrasset	Tamanrasset
27. Tébessa	Tébessa
28. Tiaret	Tiaret
29. Tizi-Ouzou	Tizi-Ouzou
30. Tlemcen	Tlemcen
31. M'Sila	M'Sila

(1) AMERICAN SAMOA

(2) American Samoa

(3) American Samoa

(4) These islands are approximately 650 miles northeast of Fiji in the Pacific.

(5) Pago Pago

(6) American Samoa comprises 19 administrative units; 4 districts and 15 counties.

Districts	Capitals
1. Eastern Tutuila	Alofau
2. Western Tutuila	Asu
3. Manu'a	Olosega
4. Swain's Island	Swain's Island

Counties	Capitals
5. Ituau	Avau
6. Mauputasi	Pago Pago
7. Saole	Utumea
8. Sua	Aumi
9. Vaifanua East	Alao
10. Lealataua	Utumea
11. Leasina	Malaeoloa
12. Tualauta	Faleniu
13. Tualatai	Taputima
14. Faleasao	Faleasao
15. Fitiuta	Maia
16. Ofu	Ofu
17. Olosega	Olosega
18. Ta'u	Luma
19. Vaifanua West	Vatia

(1) ANDORRA

(2) The Co-principality of Andorra

(3) Principat d'Andorra

(4) In the eastern Pyrenees on the French-Spanish border.

(5) Andorra-La-Vella

(6) Andorra comprises 7 administrative units known as Parishes.

Parishes	Capitals
1. Canillo	Canillo
2. Encamp	Encamp

4

3.	Ordino	Ordino
4.	Massana	Massana
5.	Sant Julià de Lorià	Sant Julià de Lorià
6.	Andorra-la-Vella	Andorra-la-Vella
7.	Les Escaldes-Engordany	Les Escaldes-Engordany

(1) ANGOLA

(2) People's Republic of Angola

(3) República Popular de Angola

(4) Bounded by Zaïre on the north and northeast, Zambia on the east, Botswana and Namibia on the south, and the Atlantic Ocean on the west.

(5) Luanda

(6) Angola comprises 18 administrative units known as provinces.

Provinces	Capitals
1. Cabinda	Cabinda
2. Zaire	São Salvador
3. Uíge	Carmona
4. Luanda	Luanda
5. Cuanza Norte	Salazar
6. Cuanza Sul	Novo Redondo
7. Malange	Malange
8. Lunda-Norte	Lukapa
9. Benguela	Benguela
10. Huamba	Nova Lisboa
11. Bié	Kuito
12. Moxico	Luso
13. Cuando-Cubango	Menongue
14. Mocâmedes	Mocâmedes
15. Huíla	Saõ da Bandeiro
16. Cunene	Roçadas
17. Lunda-Sul	**Saurimo**
18. Bengo	Caxito

(1) ANGUILLA

(2) British Dependent Territory of Anguilla

(3) British Dependent Territory of Anguilla

(4) Anguilla is the most northerly of the Leeward Islands, lying 70 miles to the northwest of St. Kitts and five miles to the north of St. Martin.

(5) The Valley

(6) Anguilla comprises 7 administrative units known as settlements.

Settlements
1. Island Harbour
2. Mount Fortune
3. Sandy Ground Village
4. Blowing Point Village
5. Long Bay Village
6. West End Village
7. The Valley

(1) ANTIGUA

(2) The British Associated State of Antigua

(3) The British Associated State of Antigua

(4) Antigua, with its dependencies of Barbuda and Redonda, lies in the Leeward Islands of the West Indies in the eastern Caribbean.

(5) St. John's

(6) Antigua comprises 7 administrative units; 6 parishes and 1 dependency

Parishes	Capitals
1. St. John's	St. John's
2. St. George	Parham
3. St. Mary	Bolands
4. St. Peter	Parham
5. St. Phillip	Carlisle
6. St. Paul	Nelson's Dockyard

The dependency is Barbuda Island, its capital is Codrington.

(1) ARGENTINA

(2) The Argentine Republic

(3) República Argentina

(4) Argentina is bounded in the north by Bolivia; in the northeast by Paraguay; in the east by Brazil, Uruguay, and the Atlantic Ocean; and in the west by Chile.

(5) Buenos Aires

(6) Argentina comprises 24 administrative units; 1 federal capital district (Buenos Aires), 1 national territory (Tierra del Fuego/Ushuaia, capital), and 22 provinces.

Provinces	Capitals
1. Buenos Aires	La Plata
2. Corrientes	Corrientes
3. Entre Ríos	Paraná
4. Chaco	Resistencia
5. Santa Fé	Santa Fé
6. Formosa	Formosa
7. Misiones	Posadas
8. Jujuy	Jujuy
9. Salta	Salta
10. Santiago del Esero	Santiago del Esero
11. Tucumán	Tucumán
12. Córdoba	Córdoba
13. La Pampa	Santa Rosa
14. San Luis	San Luis
15. Catamarca	Catamarca
16. La Rioja	La Rioja
17. Mendoza	Mendoza
18. San Juan	San Juan
19. Neuquén	Neuquén
20. Chubut	Rawson
21. Rió Negro	Viedma
22. Santa Cruz	Rio Gallegos

(1) AUSTRALIA

(2) The Commonwealth of Australia

(3) The Commonwealth of Australia

(4) Australia, including Tasmania, comprises a land continent of almost eight million square kilometers in area. It lies between latitudes 10°41' south and 43°39' south and longitudes 113°09' east and 153°39' east.

(5) Canberra

(6) Australia comprises 8 administrative units; 1 federal capital territory (Australian Capital Territory/Canberra, capital), 1 federal territory (Northern/Darwin, capital), and 6 states.

States	Capitals
1. New South Wales	Sydney
2. Victoria	Melbourne
3. Queensland	Brisbane
4. Tasmania	Hobart
5. South Australia	Adelaide
6. Western Australia	Perth

(1) AUSTRIA

(2) The Republic of Austria

(3) Republik Osterreich

(4) Austria lies in Central Europe, between Switzerland, Liechtenstein, Germany, Czechoslovakia, Hungary, Yugoslavia, and Italy.

(5) Vienna (Wien)

(6) Austria comprises 9 administrative units or "Länder."

Länder	Capitals
1. Wien	Vienna (Wien)
2. Niederösterreich	Niederösterreich
3. Burgenland	Eisenstadt
4. Oberösterreich	Linz
5. Salzburg	Salzburg
6. Steiermark	Graz
7. Kärnten	Klagenfurt
8. Tirol	Innsbruck
9. Vorarlberg	Bregenz

(1) BAHAMAS

(2) The Commonwealth of the Bahamas

(3) The Commonwealth of the Bahamas

(4) Off the southeast coast of Florida, consisting of a group of some 700 islands and over 1,000 cays.

(5) Nassau

(6) Bahamas comprises 19 administrative units or districts.

Districts	Capitals
1. Grand Bahama	Freeport
2. Harbour Island	Dunmore Town
3. Eleuthera/North	Governor's Harbour
4. Eleuthera/South	Rock Sound
5. Andros and the Berry Islands	Nicholls Town
6. Andros/Kemps Bay	Kemps Bay
7. Inagua	Matthewtown
8. Abaco/G.T.C.	Green Turtle Cay
9. Bimini	Alice Town
10. Cat Island	The Bight
11. Long Island	Clarence Town
12. Abaco/S.P.	Sandy Point
13. Crooked Island	Colonel Hill
14. Exuma	**George Town**
15. Mayaguana	Abrahams Bay
16. San Salvador	Cockburn Town
17. Ragged Island	Duncan Town
18. Andros/F.C.	Fresh Creek
19. Abaco/M.H.	Marsh Harbour

(1) BAHRAIN

(2) The Amirate of Bahrain

(3) Dawlat al-Bahrain

(4) An archipelago of islands in the Arabian Gulf, between the Qator Peninsula and the mainland of Saudi Arabia.

(5) Manama

(6) Bahrain comprises 9 administrative units known as districts.

Districts	Capitals
1. Central	Manama
2. Judhafs	Judhafs
3. Manama	Manama
4. Muharraq	Muharraq
5. (Northern) Al Hadd	Al Hadd
6. Riffa	Riffa
7. Sitrah	Sitrah
8. Western	Manama
9. Other Islands	Manama

(1) BANGLADESH

(2) The People's Republic of Bangladesh

(3) "Ganaprojatantri Bangladesh"

(4) Bangladesh is bounded on the west and northwest by the Indian
State of West Bengal, on the north by Assam and Meghalaya,
on the east by Assam, Tripura, and Burma, and on the south
by the Bay of Bengal.

(5) Dacca

(6) Bangladesh comprises 25 administrative units; 4 divisions and
21 districts.

Divisions	Capitals
1. Rajshani	Rajshani
2. Dacca	Dacca
3. Khulna	Khulna
4. **Chittigong**	**Chittigong**

Districts	Capitals
5. Dinajpur	Dinajpur
6. Rangpur	Rangpur
7. Bogra	Bogra
8. **Rajshahi**	**Rajshahi**
9. Pabna	Pabna
10. Tangail	Tangail
11. Mymensingh	Mymensingh
12. Dacca	Dacca
13. Faridpur	Faridpur
14. Kushtia	Kushtia
15. Jessore	Jessore
16. Khulna	Khulna
17. Bakerganj-Barisal	Bakerganj-Barisal
18. Putuakhali	Putuakhali
19. Sylhet	Sylhet
20. Comilla	Comilla
21. Noakhali-Feni	Noakhali-Feni
22. Chittigong	Chittigong
23. Chittigong Hill Tracts	Rangamati
24. Rangamati	Khagrachari
25. Bandarban	Bandarban

(1) BARBADOS

(2) Commonwealth of Barbados

(3) Commonwealth of Barbados

(4) A Caribbean West Indies Island which lies to the east of the Windward Islands.

(5) Bridgetown

(6) Barbados comprises 12 administrative units; 1 independent city (Bridgetown) and 11 **parishes.** (**There are** no capitals because they are administered from Bridgetown.)

Parishes
1. Christ Church
2. St. Andrew
3. St. George
4. St. James
5. St. John
6. St. Joseph
7. St. Lucy
8. St. Michael
9. St. Peter
10. St. Phillip
11. St. Thomas

(1) BELAU

(2) The Republic of Belau

(3) The Republic of Belau

(4) Belau consists of a main group of islands known as the Pelau Group and four small coral islands scattered between the Pelau Group and the northeastern islands of Indonesia.

(5) Koror, Pelau Islands

(6) Belau Republic comprises 18 administrative units known as subdivisions.

Subdivisions
1. Anguar Municipality
2. Aimelik Municipality
3. Airai Municipality
4. Melekeiok Municipality
5. Ngaraard Municipality
6. Ngaramlengui Municipality
7. Ngarchelong Municipality
8. Ngardmau Municipality
9. Ngartrang Municipality

11

10. Ngchesar Municipality
11. Ngiwal Municipality
12. Kayangel Municipality
13. Koror Municipality
14. Koror Town
15. Peleliu Munk Municipality
16. Pulu Anna Island
17. Sonsoral Municipality
18. Tobi Municipality

(1) BELGIUM

(2) The Kingdom of Belgium

(3) **Royaume** de Belgique

(4) Belgium is bounded in the north by the Netherlands, the northwest by the North Sea, the west and south by France, and the east by the Federal Republic of Germany and Luxembourg.

(5) Brussels

(6) Belgium comprises 9 administrative units known as provinces.

Provinces	Capitals
1. Antwerpen	Antwerpen
2. Brabant	Brussels
3. Hainaut	Mons
4. Liège	Liège
5. Limburg	Hasselt
6. Luxembourg	Arlon
7. Namur	Namur
8. Oost-Vlaanderen	Ghent
9. West-Vlaanderen	Bruges

(1) BELIZE

(2) Commonwealth of Belize

(3) Commonwealth of Belize

(4) Belize is a Central American country bounded in the north by Mexico, in the west by Guatemala, and in the east and south by the Caribbean Sea.

12

(5) Belmopan

(6) Belize comprises 6 administrative units known as districts.

Districts	Capitals
1. Belize	Belize
2. El Cayo	El Cayo
3. Corozal	Corozal
4. Orange Walk	Orange Walk
5. Stann Creek	Dangriga
6. Toledo	Punta Gorda

(1) BENIN

(2) The People's Republic of Benin

(3) République Populaire du Benin

(4) Benin is bounded in the east by Nigeria, in the north by Niger
      and Upper Volta, and in the west by Togo.

(5) Porto-Novo

(6) Benin comprises 45 administrative units; 6 départements, and
      39 districts.

Départements	Capitals
1. Atakora	Natitingou
2. Borgou	Parakou
3. Zou	Abomey
4. Quémé	Porto-Novo
5. Atlantique	Cotonou
6. Mono	Lokossa

Districts	Capitals
7. Kétou	Kétou
8. Pobé	Pobé
9. Adjohoun	Adjohoun
10. Sakété	Sakété
11. Dangbo	Dangbo
12. Avrankou	Avrankou
13. Houlénou	Houlénou
14. Abomey-Calavi	Abomey-Calavi
15. Ouidah	Ouidah
16. Allada	Allada
17. Grand-Popo	Grand-Popo
18. Athiémé	Athiémé
19. Klouékanmé	Klouékanmé

20. Aplahoué	Aplahoué
21. Dogbo	Dogbo
22. Bopa	Bopa
23. Cotonou	Cotonou
24. Abomey	Abomey
25. Bohicon	Bohicon
26. Zagnanado	Zagnanado
27. Dassa-Zoumé	Dassa-Zoumé
28. Savalou	Savalou
29. Savé	Savé
30. Bassila	Bassila
31. Ouaké	Ouaké
32. Djougou	Djougou
33. Boukoumbé	Boukoumbé
34. Nattingou	Nattingou
35. Kouandé	Kouandé
36. Tanguiéta	Tanguiéta
37. Kérou	Kérou
38. Malanville	Malanville
39. Banikoara	Banikoara
40. Kandi	Kandi
41. Ségbana	Ségbana
42. Bembèrèkè	Bembèrèkè
43. Nikki	Nikki
44. Parakou	Parakou
45. Porto-Novo	Porto-Novo

(1)   BERMUDA

(2)   Commonwealth of Bermuda

(3)   Commonwealth of Bermuda

(4)   A group of some 150 small islands in the western Atlantic Ocean, the nearest point on the American mainland about 570 miles from Cape Hatteras, N.C.

(5)   Hamilton

(6)   Bermuda comprises 9 administrative units known as parishes.

Parishes	Capitals
1. St. George's	St. George's
2. Smith's	The Flatts
3. Hamilton	Radnor
4. Devonshire	Aeloia
5. Pembroke	Hamilton
6. Paget	Cliff Lodge

7.	Warwick	Granaway
8.	Southampton	Cedarhurst
9.	Sandys	Somerset

(1) BHUTAN

(2) The Kingdom of Bhután

(3) Druk-Yul

(4) Bhutan is situated in the eastern Himalayas, bordered on the north and east by Tibet and India, on the west by Sikkim, and on the south by India.

(5) Thimphu

(6) Bhutan comprises 15 administrative units known as districts or "Dzongs."

Dzongs	Capitals
1. Shingbe	Shingbe
2. Tashi Gang	Tashi Gang
3. Dewagiri	Dewagiri
4. Thunkar	Thunkar
5. Tongsa	Tongsa
6. Punakha	Punakha
7. Wangdu Phrodang	Wangdu Phrodang
8. Phunchholing	Phunchholing
9. Paro	Paro
10. Thimbu	Thimbu
11. Lingshi	Lingshi
12. Chekha	Chekha
13. Ha	Ha
14. Tashi Chhö	Tashi Chhö
15. Byakar	Byakar

(1) BOLIVIA

(2) Republic of Bolivia

(3) República de Bolivia

(4) A landlocked state in South America, bounded on the north and east by Brazil, on the south by Paraguay and Argentina, and on the west by Chile and Peru.

15

(5) La Paz

(6) Bolivia comprises 108 administrative units; 9 departments and
     99 provinces.

Departments	Capitals
1. La Paz	La Paz
2. Cochabamba	Cochabamba
3. Potsí	Potsí
4. Santa Cruz	Santa Cruz
5. Chuquisaca	Sucre
6. Tarija	Tarija
7. Oruro	Oruro
8. Beni	Trinidad
9. Pando	Cobija

Provinces	Capitals
10. Oropeza	Oropeza
11. Azurduy	Azurduy
12. Zudañez	Zudañez
13. Tomina	Tomina
14. Hernando Siles	Hernando Siles
15. Yamparaez	Yamparaez
16. Nor Cinti	Nor Cinti
17. Belisario Boeto	Belisario Boeto
18. Sud Cinti	Sud Cinti
19. Luis Calvo	Luis Calvo
20. Murillo	Murillo
21. Omasuyos	Omasuyos
22. Pacajes	Pacajes
23. Camacho	Camacho
24. Muñecas	Muñecas
25. Larecaja	Larecaja
26. Franz Tamayo	Franz Tamayo
27. Ingavi	Ingavi
28. Loayza	Loayza
29. Inquisivi	Inquisivi
30. Sud Yungas	Sud Yungas
31. Los Andes	Los Andes
32. Aroma	Aroma
33. Nor Yungas	Nor Yungas
34. Abel Iturralde	Abel Iturralde
35. Bautista Saavedra	Bautista Saavedra
36. Manco Kapac	Manco Kapac
37. Gualberto Villarroel	Gualberto Villarroel
38. Cercado (Cochabamba)	Cercado (Cochabamba)
39. Campero	Campero
40. Ayopaya	Ayopaya
41. Esteban Arce	Esteban Arce
42. Arani	Arani
43. Arque	Arque

44.	Capinota	Capinota
45.	Jordán	Jordán
46.	Quillacollo	Quillacollo
47.	Chapare	Chapare
48.	Tapacarí	Tapacarí
49.	Carrasco	Carrasco
50.	Mizque	Mizque
51.	Punata	Punata
52.	Cercado (Oruro)	Cercado (Oruro)
53.	Avaroa	Avaroa
54.	Carangas	Carangas
55.	Sajama	Sajama
56.	Litoral	Litoral
57.	Poopó	Poopó
58.	Pantaleón Dalence	Pantaleón Dalence
59.	Ladislao Cabrera	Ladislao Cabrera
60.	Atahuallpa	Atahuallpa
61.	Saucari	Saucari
62.	Frías	Frías
63.	Bustillos	Bustillos
64.	Cornelio Saavedra	Cornelio Saavedra
65.	Chayanta	Chayanta
66.	Charcas	Charcas
67.	Nur Chichas	Nur Chichas
68.	Alonso de Ibañez	Alonso de Ibañez
69.	Sud Chichas	Sud Chichas
70.	Nor Lípez	Nor Lípez
71.	Sud Lípez	Sud Lípez
72.	Linares	Linares
73.	Quijarro	Quijarro
74.	Gral. Bilbao	Gral. Bilbao
75.	Daniel Campos	Daniel Campos
76.	Modesto Omiste	Modesto Omiste
77.	Gral. F. Román	Gral. F. Román
78.	Cercado (Tarija)	Cercado (Tarija)
79.	Arce	Arce
80.	Gran Chaco	Gran Chaco
81.	Aviléz	Aviléz
82.	Méndez	Méndez
83.	O'Connor	O'Connor
84.	Andrés/Bañez	Andrés/Bañez
85.	Warnes	Warnes
86.	Velasco	Velasco
87.	Ichilo	Ichilo
88.	Chiquitos	Chiquitos
89.	Sarah	Sarah
90.	Cordillera	Cordillera
91.	Vallegrande	Vallegrande
92.	Florida	Florida
93.	Obispo Santiesteban	Obispo Santiesteban
94.	Ñuflo de Chavez	Ñuflo de Chavez

95.	Angél Sandoval		Angél Sandoval
96.	Manuel María Caballero		Manuel María Caballero
97.	Cercado (Bení)		Cercado (Bení)
98.	Vaca Diez		Vaca Diez
99.	Gral. Ballivian		Gral. Ballivian
100.	Yacuma		Yacuma
101.	Moxos		Moxos
102.	Marbán		Marbán
103.	Mamoré		Mamoré
104.	Itenez		Itenez
105.	Nicolas Suárez		Nicolas Suárez
106.	Manuripi		Manuripi
107.	Madre de Dios		Madre de Dios
108.	Abuná		Abuná

(1) BOTSWANA

(2) The Republic of Botswana

(3) The Republic of Botswana

(4) Botswana is an African country lying between the Molopa and Zambezi Rivers, and extending from South Africa and Zimbabwe on the east to **Namibia on the west.**

(5) Gaborone

(6) Botswana comprises 13 administrative units; 4 independent towns and 9 districts.

Independent Towns
1. Gaborone
2. Francistown
3. Selebi-Pikwe
4. Lobatse

Districts		Capitals
5.	Ngwato	Serowe
6.	Ghanzi	Ghanzi
7.	Kgalagadi	Tshabong
8.	Kgatleng	Mochudi
9.	Kweneng	Molepolole
10.	North East	Francistown
11.	North West	Maun
12.	Ngwaketse	Kanye
13.	South East	Ramotswa

(1) BRAZIL

(2) The Federated Republic of Brazil

(3) República Federativa do Brasil

(4) Brazil is bounded by the Atlantic on the east, and on its northwest and southern borders by all of the South American countries except Chile and Ecuador.

(5) Brasilia

(6) Brazil comprises 27 administrative units; 1 federal capital district (Distrito Federal/Brasilia, capital), 4 Federal Territories known as "Territórios" and 22 states known as "estados."

Federal Territories	Capitals
1. Rondônia	Pôrto Velho
2. Fernando de Noronha	Fernando de Noronha
3. Roraima	Boa Vista
4. Amapá	Macapá

States	Capitals
5. Acre	Rio Branco
6. Amazonas	Manaus
7. Pará	Bélem
8. Maranhão	São Luis
9. Piauí	Teresina
10. Ceará	Fortaleza
11. Rio Grande do Norte	Natal
12. Paraíba	João Pessoa
13. Pernambuco	Recife
14. Alagoas	Maceió
15. Sergipe	Aracajú
16. Bahia	Salvador
17. Minas Gerais	Belo Horizonte
18. Espírito Santo	Vitória
19. Rio de Janeiro	Rio de Janeiro
20. São Paulo	São Paulo
21. Paraná	Curtiba
22. Santa Catarina	Flurianópolis
23. Rio Grande do Sul	Pórto Alegre
24. Matto Grosso	Cuiabá
25. Goiás	Goiânia
26. Matto Grosso **Do Sul**	Campo Grande

(1) BRITISH INDIAN OCEAN TERRITORY

(2) British Indian Ocean Territory

(3) British Indian Ocean Territory

(4) The British Indian Ocean Territory is a territorial grouping of four coral atolls in the Seychelles Islands of the Indian Ocean. They are: Diego Garcia, Aldabra, Desroches, and Faraquhar.

(5) Diego Garcia

(6) British Indian Ocean Territory comprises 3 administrative units known as Natural Regions. They are: Diego Garcia, Peros Banhos, and Salomon.

(1) BRITISH VIRGIN ISLANDS

(2) Crown Colony of the British Virgin Islands

(3) Crown Colony of the British Virgin Islands

(4) The British Virgin Islands are a group of 42 islands at the eastern extremity of the Greater Antilles. They have a total land area of 59 square miles.

(5) Roadtown

(6) British Virgin Islands comprise 4 administrative units known as island councils.

Councils	Capitals
1. Tortola	Roadtown
2. Virgin Gorda	North Sound
3. Anegada	The Settlement
4. Jost Van Dyke	Great Harbour Bay

(1) BRUNEI

(2) The State of Brunei

(3) Negeri Brunei

(4) On the northwest coast of Borneo, Brunei is bounded on all

sides by Malaysian Sarawak territory, which splits the Sultanate into two separate parts.

(5) Bandar Seri Begawan

(6) Brunei comprises 4 administrative units known as districts.

Districts	Capitals
1. Brunei/Muara	Bandar Seri Begawan
2. Seria/Kuala Belait	Kuala Belait
3. Tutong	Tutong
4. Temburong	Temburong

(1) BULGARIA

(2) The People's Republic of Bulgaria

(3) Narodna Republika Bugaria

(4) Bulgaria is bounded in the north by Romania, on the east by
the Black Sea, on the south by Turkey and Greece, and on
the west by Yugoslavia.

(5) Sofia

(6) Bulgaria comprises 28 administrative units known as districts
or "Okrug."

Okrug	Capitals
1. Blagoevgrad	Blagoevgrad
2. Burgas	Burgas
3. Gabrovo	Gabrovo
4. Khaskovo	Khaskovo
5. Kŭrdzhali	Kŭrdzhali
6. Kyustendil	Kyustendil
7. Lovech	Lovech
8. Mikhailovgrad	Mikhailovgrad
9. Pazardzhik	Pazardzhik
10. Pernik	Pernik
11. Plevin	Plevin
12. Plovdiv	Plovdiv
13. Razgrad	Razgrad
14. Russe	Russe
15. Shumen	Shumen
16. Silistra	Silistra
17. Sliven	Sliven
18. Smolyan	Smolyan
19. Sofia (Okrug)	Sofia (Okrug)

20. Sofia (City)	Sofia (City)
21. Stara Zagora	Stara Zagora
22. Tolbukhin	Tolbukhin
23. Tŭrgovishte	Tŭrgovishte
24. Varna	Varna
25. Veliko Tŭrnovo	Turnovo
26. Vidin	Vidin
27. Vratsa	Vratsa
28. Yambol	Yambol

(1) BURMA

(2) The Socialist Republic of the Union of Burma

(3) Pyidaungsu Socialist Thammada Myanma Naingngandaw

(4) Burma is bounded in the east by China, Laos, and Thailand, and in the west by the Indian Ocean, Bangladesh, and India.

(5) Rangoon

(6) Burma comprises 14 administrative units; 7 states and 7 divisions.

States	Capitals
1. Chin	Haka
2. Mon	Moulmein
3. Shan	Taunggyi
4. Kayah	Loikaw
5. Kachin	Myitkyina
6. Karen	Pa-An
7. Arakan	Akyab

Divisions	Capitals
8. Rangoon	Rangoon
9. Pegu	Pegu
10. Tenasserim	Tavoy
11. Mandalay	Mandalay
12. Magwe	Magwe
13. Irrawaddy	Bassein
14. Sagaing	Sagaing

(1) BURUNDI

(2) Republic of Burundi

(3)   République du Burundi

(4)   Burundi lies astride the main African Nile-Congo dividing crest
      and is bounded on the west by the narrow plain of the Ruzizi
      River and Lake Tanganyika.

(5)   Bujumbura

(6)   Burundi comprises 8 administrative units known as provinces.

Provinces	Capitals
1. Bujumbura	Bujumbura
2. Bubanza	Bubanza
3. Muramvya	Muramvya
4. Ngozi	Ngozi
5. Kitega	Kitega
6. Muhinga	Muhinga
7. Ruyigi	Ruyigi
8. Bururi	Bururi

(1)   CAMEROON

(2)   The United Republic of Cameroon

(3)   République Unie du Cameroun

(4)   Cameroon is bounded on the west by the Bight of Bonny, on
      the northwest by Nigeria, and on the northeast by Chad,
      with Lake Chad at its northern tip.

(5)   Yaoundé

(6)   Cameroon comprises 43 administrative units; 7 provinces and
      36 départements.

Provinces	Capitals
1. Centre-Sud	Yaoundé
2. Littoral	Douala
3. Ouest	Bafoussam
4. Sud-Ouest	Buea
5. Nord-Ouest	Bamenda
6. Nord	Garoua
7. Est	Bertoua

Départements	Capitals
8. Dja-et-Lobo	Sangmélima
9. Haute-Sanga	Nanga-Eboko
10. Kribi	Kribi

23

11.	Lékié	Obala
12.	Mbam	Bafia
13.	Méfou	Yaoundé
14.	Ntem	Ebolowe
15.	Nyong-et-Kélé	Eséka
16.	Nyong-et-Mfoumou	Akonolinga
17.	Nyong-et-Soo	Mbalmayo
18.	Boumba-Ngoko	Yokadouma
19.	Haute-Nyong	Abong Mbang
20.	Kadeï	Batouri
21.	Lom-et-Djerem	Bertoua
22.	Mungo	Nkongsamba
23.	Nkam	Yabassi
24.	Sanaga-Maritîme	Edea
25.	Wouri	Douala
26.	Adamaoua	Adamaoua
27.	Bénoué	Garoua
28.	Diamaré	Maroua
29.	Logone-et-Chari	Fort-Foureau
30.	Margui-Wandala	Mokolo
31.	Mayo-Danaï	Yagoua
32.	Bamboutos	Mbouda
33.	Bamoun	Foumban
34.	Haut-Nkam	Bafang
35.	Ménoua	Dschang
36.	Mifi	Bafoussam
37.	Ndé	Bangangté
38.	Bamenda	Bamenda
39.	Kumba	Kumba
40.	Mamfe	Mamfe
41.	Nkambe	Nkambe
42.	Victoria	Victoria
43.	Wum	Wum

(1)   CANADA

(2)   The Dominion of Canada

(3)   The Dominion of Canada

(4)   Canada occupies the northern part of North America, with the
      U.S.A. on its southern border, along the 49th parallel. Its
      western border is the Pacific Ocean and its eastern border
      is the Atlantic Ocean.

(5)   Ottawa

(6)   Canada comprises 12 administrative units; 2 federal territories
      and 10 provinces.

24

Federal Territories	Capitals
1. Yukon	Whitehorse
2. Northwest	Yellowknife

Provinces	Capitals
3. Newfoundland	St. John's
4. Prince Edward Island	Charlottetown
5. Nova Scotia	Halifax
6. New Brunswick	Fredericton
7. Quebec	Quebec City
8. Ontario	Toronto
9. Manitoba	Winnipeg
10. Saskatchewan	Regina
11. Alberta	Edmonton
12. British Columbia	Victoria

(1) CAPE VERDE

(2) Republic of Cape Verde

(3) República de Cabo Verde

(4) Cape Verde is situated in the Atlantic Ocean 350 miles WNW of Senegal and consists of ten islands and five islets.

(5) Praia

(6) Cape Verde comprises 14 administrative units known as divisions or "concelhos."

Concelhos	Capitals
1. Boa Vista	Sal-Rei
2. Brava	Nova Sintra
3. Fogo	São Felipe
4. Maio	Maio
5. Paúl	Porto Novo
6. Porto Novo	Porto Novo
7. Praia	Praia
8. Ribeira Grande	Ribeira Grande
9. Sal	Santa Mara
10. Santa Catarina	Santa Catarina
11. Santa Cruz	Santa Cruz
12. São Nicolau	Villa de Ribeira Bravo
13. São Luzia	Mindefo
14. Tarrafal	Tarrafal

(1) CAYMAN ISLANDS

(2) Cayman Islands

(3) Cayman Islands

(4) Cayman Islands are situated in the Caribbean Sea, about 200 miles NW of Jamaica.

(5) Georgetown

(6) The Cayman Islands comprise 11 administrative units; 4 districts, Cayman Brac, 5 districts, Grand Cayman, and 2 districts, Little Cayman.

> Districts, Cayman Brac
> 1. Creer
> 2. Spot Bay
> 3. Stake Bay
> 4. West End
>
> Districts, Grand Cayman
> 5. Georgetown
> 6. Bodden Town
> 7. East End
> 8. West Bay
> 9. North Side
>
> Districts, Little Cayman
> 10. South Town
> 11. Jacksons

(1) CENTRAL AFRICAN REPUBLIC

(2) The Central African Republic

(3) La République Centrafricaine

(4) The Central African Republic is bounded in the north by Chad, in the east by Sudan, in the south by Zaïre, and in the west by Cameroon.

(5) Bangui

(6) Central African Republic comprises 15 administrative units; 1 capital commune (Bangui) and 14 prefectures.

26

Prefecture	Capitals
1. Ombella-M'Poko	Bangui
2. Birao	Birao
3. Bouar-Baboua	Bouar
4. Kémo-Gribingui	Fort-Sibut
5. Basse-Kotto	Mobaye
6. Haute-Kotto	Bria
7. Lobaye	M'Baiki
8. M'Bomou	Bangassou
9. N'Dele	N'Dele
10. Obo-Zemio	Obo
11. Ouaka	Bambari
12. Ouham	Bassangoa
13. Ouham-Pendé	Bozoum
14. Haute-Sangha	Berbérati

(1) CHAD

(2) The Republic of Chad

(3) République du Tchad

(4) Chad is bounded in the north by Libya, in the east by Sudan, and in the south by the Central African Republic.

(5) N'Djamena

(6) Chad comprises 14 administrative units known as prefectures.

Prefectures	Capitals
1. Batha	Ati
2. Biltine	Biltine
3. Borkou-Ennedi-Tibesti	Faya-Largeau
4. Chari-Banguirmi	N'Djamena
5. Guéra	Mongo
6. Kanem	Mao
7. Lac	Bol
8. Logone Occidental	Moundou
9. Logone Oriental	Doba
10. Mayo-Kebbi	Bongor
11. Moyen-Chari	Fort Archambault
12. Oudaï	Abèché
13. Salamat	Am-Timan
14. Tandjilé	Laï

(1)   CHANNEL ISLAND OF GUERNSEY

(2)   Channel Island of Guernsey

(3)   Channel Island of Guernsey

(4)   Guernsey lies to the northwest of Jersey, off the northwest coast of France. Guernsey's dependencies consist of seven other islands.

(5)   St. Peter Port

Guernsey (The Channel Islands) **comprises** 14 administrative units; 10 parishes and 4 adjacent islands (dependencies).

<u>Parishes</u>
1. Castel
2. Forest
3. St. Andrew
4. St. Martin
5. St. Peter-in-the-Wood
6. St. Peter Port
7. St. Sampson
8. St. Saviour
9. Torteval
10. Vale

<u>Adjacent Islands</u>		Capitals
11.	Alderney	St. Anne's
12.	Herm	Shell Beach
13.	Jethou	Jethou
14.	Sark	Creux

(1)   CHANNEL ISLAND OF JERSEY

(2)   Channel Island of Jersey

(3)   Channel Island of Jersey

(4)   Jersey, the largest of the Channel Islands, is situated to the southeast of Guernsey, from which it is separated by seventeen miles of sea. Both islands lie off the northwest coast of France.

(5)   St. Helier

(6)   Jersey (The **Channel** Islands) comprises 12 administrative units known as parishes.

Parishes
1. Grouville
2. St. Brelade
3. St. Clement
4. St. Hélier
5. St. John
6. St. Lawrence
7. St. Martin
8. St. Mary
9. St. Peter
10. St. Saviour
11. St. Ouen
12. Trinity

(1) CHILE

(2) Republic of Chile

(3) República de Chile

(4) Chile is bounded in the north by Peru, in the east by Bolivia and Argentina, and in the west by the Pacific Ocean.

(5) Santiago

(6) Chile comprises 53 administrative units; 1 federal capital district (Metropolitan Region/Santiago, capital), 12 administrative regions, and 40 provinces.

Administrative Regions	Capitals
1. Tarapacá	Iquiqe
2. Antofagasta	Antofagasta
3. Coquimbo	La Serena
4. Aconcagua	Valparaíso
5. Del Maule	Talca
6. Del Libertador Gen. Bernardo O'Higgins	Rancagua
7. Bíobío	Concepción
8. De La Araucanía	Temuco
9. De Los Lagos	Puerto Montt
10. **Aisén del Gen. Carlos** Ibáñez del Campo	Coihaique
11. Magallanes y Antártica Chilena	Punta Arenas
12. Atacama	Copiapó

Provinces	Capitals
13. Arica	Arica

14. Iquique	Iquique
15. Tocopilla	Tocopilla
16. El Loa	Calama
17. Antofagasta	Antofagasta
18. Chañaral	Chañaral
19. Copiapó	Copiapó
20. Huasco	Vallenar
21. Elqui	Coquimbo
22. Límarí	Ovalle
23. Choapa	Illapel
24. Peturca	La Ligua
25. San Felipe	San Felipe
26. Los Andes	Los Andes
27. Valparaíso	Valparaíso
28. Quillota	Quillota
29. San Antonio	San Antonio
30. Isla de Pascua	Hangaroa
31. Cachapoal	Rancagua
32. Colchagua	San Fernando
33. Curicó	Curicó
34. Talca	Talca
35. Linares	Linares
36. Ñuble	Chillán
37. Concepción	Concepción
38. Biobío	Los Angeles
39. Arauco	Lebu
40. Malleco	Angol
41. Cautín	Temuco
42. Valdivia	Valdivia
43. Osorno	Osorno
44. Llanquihue	Puerto Montt
45. Aisén	Coihaique
46. General Carrera	Chile Chico
47. Capitán Prat	Cochrane
48. Altima Esperanza	Puerto Natales
49. Magallanes	Punta Arenas
50. Antártica Chilena	Puerto Williams
51. Tierra Del Fuego	Porvenir
52. Chiloe	Castro

(1) CHINA, (MAINLAND)

(2) People's Republic of China

(3) Zhonghua Renmin Gongheguo

(4) Mainland China is bounded in the north by the U.S.S.R. and
     Mongolia; in the east by Korea, the Yellow Sea, and the East

China Sea; in the south by Vietnam, Laos, Burma, India, Bhutan, and Nepal; and in the west by India, Pakistan, Afghanistan, and the U.S.S.R.

(5) Peking (Beijing)

(6) China comprises 30 administrative units; 3 national municipalities, 5 autonomous regions, and 22 provinces.

National Municipalities
1. Beijing (Peking)
2. Shanghai
3. Tianjin

Autonomous Regions	Capitals
4. Guangxi Zhuang	Nanning
5. Nei Monggol	Hohhot
6. Xinjiang Uygur	Urumqi
7. Ningxia Hui	Yinchuan
8. Xizag (Tibet)	Lhasa

Provinces	Capitals
9. Sichuan	Chengdu
10. Shandong	Jinan
11. Henan	Zhengzhou
12. Jiangsu	Nanjing
13. Hebei	Tianjin
14. Guangdong	Guangzhou
15. Hunan	Changsha
16. Anhui	Hefei
17. Hubei	Wuhan
18. Zhejiang	Hangzhou
19. Liaoning	Shenyang
20. Yunnan	Kunming
21. Jiangxi	Nanchang
22. Shaanxi	Xian
23. Heilongjiang	Harbin
24. Shanxi	Taiyuan
25. Guizhou	Guiyang
26. Fujian	Fuzhou
27. Jilin	Changchun
28. Gansu	Lanzhou
29. Qinghai	Xining
30. Taiwan	Taipeh

(1) CHINA (TAIWAN)

(2) Republic of China

(3) Republic of China

(4) The island of Taiwan (formerly Formosa) lies between the East
     and South China Seas off the coast of Mainland China's Fukien
     Province.

(5) Taipei

(6) China (Taiwan) comprises 21 administrative units; 1 capital
     municipality (Taipeh), 4 independent municipalities, and 16
     counties or "Hsien."

Independent Municipalities
   1. Kaohsiung
   2. Keelung
   3. Taichung
   4. Tainan

Hsien		Capitals
5.	Taipeh	Panchiao
6.	Ilan	Ilan
7.	Taoyuan	Taoyuan
8.	Hsinchu	Hsinchu
9.	Miaoli	Miaoli
10.	Taichung	Fengyuan
11.	Changhua	Changhua
12.	Nantou	Nantou
13.	Yunlin	Touliu
14.	Chiayi	Chiayi
15.	Tainan	Hsinying
16.	Kaohsiung	Fengshan
17.	Pingtung	Pingtung
18.	Taitung	Taitung
19.	Hualien	Hualien
20.	Penghu	Makung

(1) CHRISTMAS ISLAND (AUSTRALIA)

(2) Australian Territory of Christmas Island

(3) Australian Territory of Christmas Island

(4) The Christmas Island territory is situated in the Indian Ocean
     about 224 miles south of Java Head. It has an area of 52
     square miles. It lies at the south entrance to Sunda Straight,
     in lat. 10°25'S, long. 105°40'E.

(5) Flying Fish Cove

(6) Currently Christmas Island has only central administration, at the village of Flying Fish Cove.

(1) COCOS ISLANDS

(2) Australian Territory of the Cocos Islands

(3) Australian Territory of the Cocos Islands

(4) Cocos Islands are two separate atolls comprising some 27 small coral islands with a total area of about five-and-one-half square miles, situated in the Indian Ocean in latitude 12°5' south and longitude 96°53' east.

(5) West Island

(6) Cocos Islands comprise 5 administrative units known as districts.

Districts
1. West Island
2. Home Island
3. Direction Island
4. South Island
5. Horsburgh Island

(1) COLOMBIA

(2) Republic of Colombia

(3) República de Colombia

(4) Colombia is bounded in the north by the Caribbean Sea, in the northwest by Panama, in the west by the Pacific Ocean, in the southwest by Ecuador and Peru, in the northeast by Venezuela, and in the southeast by Brazil.

(5) Bogata

(6) Colombia comprises 32 administrative units; 1 special capital district (Bogata), 4 commissaries, 5 intendancies, and 22 departments.

Commissaries	Capitals
1. Amazonas	Leticia

2.	Guainía	San Felipe
3.	Vaupes	Mitú
4.	Vichada	Puerto Carreño

Intendancies		Capitals
5.	San Andés y Providencia	San Andés
6.	Casanare	Yopal
7.	Arauca	Arauca
8.	Caqueta	Florencia
9.	Putumayo	Mocoa

Departments		Capitals
10.	Antioquia	Medellín
11.	Atlántico	Barranquilla
12.	Bolívar	Cartagena
13.	Boyacá	Tunja
14.	Caldas	Manizales
15.	Cauca	Popayán
16.	César	Valledupar
17.	Córdoba	Monteria
18.	Cundinamarca	Bogatá
19.	Chocó	Quibdó
20.	Huila	Riohacha
21.	Guajira	Neiva
22.	Magdalena	Santa Marta
23.	Meta	Villavicencio
24.	Nariño	Pasto
25.	Norte de Santandar	Cúcuta
26.	Quindío	Armenia
27.	Risaralda	Pereira
28.	Santander	Bucaramanga
29.	Sucre	Sincelejo
30.	Tolima	Ibagué
31.	Valle del Cauca	Cali

(1)   COMOROS

(2)   The Federal Islamic Republic of The Comoros State

(3)   "Jumhūrīyat al Qumur al Ittihādīyah as Islamīyāh"

(4)   The Comoros are a three-island archipelago about 310 miles off the coast of Madagascar in the Indian Ocean.

(5)   Moroni

(6)   Comoros **comprise 3 administrative units** known as island districts.

Island Districts	Capitals
1. Njazidja	Moroni
2. Nzwani	Mutsamudu
3. Mwali	Fomboni

(1)   CONGO

(2)   People's Republic of The Congo

(3)   République Populaire du Congo

(4)   The Congo runs north from the Atlantic to Cameroon and the Central African Republic. To the east is Zaïre. Gabon lies to the west.

(5)   Brazzaville

(6)   Congo comprises 10 administrative units; 1 national capital district (Brazzaville), 9 "Régions" (Popular Regional Councils).

Régions	Capitals
1. Niari	Dolisie
2. Kouilou	Pointe Noire
3. Lekoumou	Sibiti
4. Bouenza	Madingou
5. Pool	Brazzaville
6. Plateaux	Djambala
7. Cuvette	Fort-Rousset
8. Sangha	Ouesso
9. Likouala	Impfondo

(1)   COOK ISLANDS

(2)   The Cook Islands Self-Governing Overseas Territory of N.Z.

(3)   The Cook Islands Self-Governing Overseas Territory of N.Z.

(4)   The Cook Islands lie in the Pacific between 8° and 23° south latitude and 156° and 167° west longitude.

(5)   Avarua

(6)   The **Cook Islands comprise** 15 administrative units known as island councils.

Island Councils	Capitals
1. Rarotonga	Rarotonga
2. Palmerston	Palmerston
3. Aitutaki	Aitutaki
4. Manuae	Manuae
5. Atiu	Atiu
6. Mangaia	Mangaia
7. Manihiki	Manihiki
8. Mauke	Mauke
9. Mitiaro	Mitiaro
10. Penrhyn	Penrhyn
11. Rakahanga	Rakahanga
12. Pukapuka	Pukapuka
13. Nassau	Nassau
14. Suwarrow	Suwarrow
15. Takutea	Takutea

(1) COSTA RICA

(2) Republic of Costa Rica

(3) República de Costa Rica

(4) Costa Rica is the most southerly state of Central America. It lies between Nicaragua and Panama, and between the Caribbean Sea and the Pacific Ocean.

(5) San José

(6) Costa Rica comprises 83 administrative units; 7 provinces and 76 cantons ("Cantones").

Provinces	Capitals
1. Alajuela	Alajuela
2. Cartago	Cartago
3. Guanacaste	Liberia
4. Heredia	Heredia
5. Limón	Limón
6. Puntarenas	Puntarenas
7. San José	San José

Cantons	Capitals
8. Central (San Jose)	San Jose
9. Escazu	Escazu
10. Desamparados	Desamparados
11. Puriscal	Puriscal
12. Tarrazu	Tarrazu
13. Aserri	Aserri

14.	Mora	Mora
15.	Goicoechea	Goicoechea
16.	Santa Ana	Santa Ana
17.	Alajuelita	Alajuelita
18.	Coronado	Coronado
19.	Acosta	Acosta
20.	Tibas	Tibas
21.	Moravia	Moravia
22.	Montes de Oca	Montes de Oca
23.	Tarrubares	Tarrubares
24.	Dota	Dota
25.	Curridabat	Curridabat
26.	Perez Zeledón	Perez Zeledón
27.	León Cortés	León Cortés
28.	Central (Alajuela)	Alajuela
29.	San Ramón	San Ramón
30.	Grecia	Grecia
31.	San Mateo	San Mateo
32.	Atenas	Atenas
33.	Naranjo	Naranjo
34.	Palmares	Palmares
35.	Poás	Poás
36.	Orotina	Orotina
37.	San Carlos	San Carlos
38.	Alfaro Ruíz	Alfaro Ruíz
39.	Valverde Vega	Valverde Vega
40.	Upala	Upala
41.	Los Chiles	Los Chiles
42.	Guatuso	Guatuso
43.	Central (Cartago)	Cartago
44.	Paraíso	Paraíso
45.	La Union	La Union
46.	Jiménez	Jiménez
47.	Turrialba	Turrialba
48.	Alvarado	Alvarado
49.	Oreamundo	Oreamundo
50.	El Guarco	El Guarco
51.	Central (Heredia)	Heredia
52.	Barba	Barba
53.	Santo Domingo	Santo Domingo
54.	Santa Barbara	Santa Barbara
55.	San Rafael	San Rafael
56.	San Isidro	San Isidro
57.	Belén	Belén
58.	Flores	Flores
59.	San Pablo	San Pablo
60.	Sarapiquí	Sarapiquí
61.	Liberia	Liberia
62.	Nicoya	Nicoya
63.	Santa Cruz	Santa Cruz
64.	Bagaces	Bagaces

65.	Carrillo	Carrillo
66.	Cañas	Cañas
67.	Abangares	Abangares
68.	Tilaran	Tilaran
69.	Nandayure	Nandayure
70.	La Cruz	La Cruz
71.	Central (Puntarenas)	Puntarenas
72.	Esparta	Esparta
73.	Buenos Aires	Buenos Aires
74.	Montes de Ora	Montes de Ora
75.	Osa	Osa
76.	Aguirre	Aguirre
77.	Golfito	Golfito
78.	Coto Brus	Coto Brus
79.	Central (Limon)	Limon
80.	Pococí	Pococí
81.	Siquirres	Siquirres
82.	Talamanca	Talamanca
83.	Matina	Matina

(1)   CUBA

(2)   Republic of Cuba

(3)   República de Cuba

(4)   The island of Cuba forms the largest and most westerly of the
Greater Antilles group and lies 135 miles south of the tip of
Florida.

(5)   Havana

(6)   Cuba comprises 14 administrative units known as provinces.

Provinces	Capitals
1. Pinar del Río	Pinar del Río
2. La Habana	Guira de Melena
3. Ciudad de la Habana	Ciudad de la Habana
4. Matanzas	Matanzas
5. Villa Clara	Santa Clara
6. Cienfuegos	Cienfuegos
7. Sancti Spíritus	Sancti Spíritus
8. Ciego de Avila	Ciego de Avila
9. Camagüey	Camagüey
10. Las Tunas	Victoria de las Tunas
11. Holguín	Holguín
12. Granma	Bayamo
13. Santiago de Cuba	Santiago de Cuba
14. Guantánamo	Guantánamo

(1) CYPRUS

(2) Democratic Republic of Cyprus

(3) Kypriaki Dimokratia

(4) The island lies in the eastern Mediterranean about 50 miles off the southern coast of Turkey and 65 miles off the coast of Syria.

(5) Nicosia

(6) Cyprus comprises 8 administrative units; 6 districts and 2 British sovereign base areas.

Districts	Capitals
1. Nicosia	Nicosia
2. Limassol	Limassol
3. Famagusta	Famagusta
4. Larnaca	Larnaca
5. Paphos	Paphos
6. Kyrenia	Kyrenia

British Bases	Capitals
7. Akrotiri	Akrotiri
8. Dhekalia	Episkopi

(1) CYPRUS (TURKISH)

(2) Turkish Federated State of Cyprus

(3) Kibris Türk Federe Devleti

(4) The northern occupied sector of the island of Cyrpus, north of the so-called "green line," constitutes Turkish Cyprus.

(5) Nicosia

(6) Turkish Cyprus comprises 4 administrative units known as districts.

Districts	Capitals
1. Kyrenia	Kyrenia
2. Nicosia	Nicosia
3. Famagusta	Famagusta
4. Laraca	Laraca

(1) CZECHOSLOVAKIA

(2) Czechoslovak Socialist Republic

(3) Československá Socialistická Republika

(4) Czechoslovakia is located in east-central Europe. It is bounded by West Germany on the southwest and west; by East Germany on the northwest and north; by the U.S.S.R. on the east; and by Austria and Hungary on the south.

(5) Prague

(6) Czechoslovakia comprises 14 administrative units; 2 national governments or "Republiky" and 12 regions or "Kraje."

National Governments	Capitals
1. Czech Socialist Republic	Praha
2. Slovak Socialist Republic	Bratislava

Regions	Capitals
3. Praha	Praha
4. Jihomoravský	Brno
5. Středočeský	Praha
6. Jihočeský	České Budejovice
7. Západočeský	Plzeň
8. Severočeský	Ústí nad Labem
9. Východočeský	Hradec Králové
10. Severomoravský	Ostrava
11. Bratislava	Bratislava
12. Západoslovenský	Bratislava
13. Středoslovenský	Baská Bystrica
14. Východoslovenský	Košice

(1) DENMARK

(2) The Danish Realm

(3) Kongeriget Danmark

(4) Denmark is located in northwestern Europe. It is bounded by the North Sea on the west; by Norway on the north; by Sweden on the east; and by West Germany on the south.

(5) Copenhagen

(6) Denmark comprises 16 administrative units; 2 special municipalities or "Kommuner" and 14 counties or "Ampter."

Kommuner
1. København
2. Frederiksborg

Ampter	Capitals
3. København	København
4. Frederiksborg	Frederiksborg
5. Roskilde	Roskilde
6. Vestsjaellands	Sorø
7. Storstøms	Nykøbing Falster
8. Bornholms	Rønne
9. Fyns	Odense
10. Sønderjyllands	Åbenrå
11. Ribe	Ribe
12. Vejle	Vejle
13. Ringkøbing	Ringkøbing
14. Åarhus	Åarhus
15. Viborg	Viborg
16. Nordjyllands	Ålborg

(1)   DJIBOUTI

(2)   Republic of Djibouti

(3)   République de Djibouti

(4)   Djibouti is situated in the Gulf of Aden between Somalia and Ethiopia.

(5)   **Djibouti**

(6)   **Djibouti comprises 5 administrative units** known as cercles.

Cercles	Capitals
1. Ali Sahih	Ali Sahih
2. Dikhil	Dikhil
3. Djibouti	Djibouti
4. Obock	Obock
5. Tadjoura	Tadjoura

(1)   DOMINICA

(2)   The Commonwealth of Dominica

(3)   The Commonwealth of Dominica

41

(4)   Dominica is an island in the Windward Group of the West Indies, between Martinique and Guadeloupe.

(5)   Roseau

(6)   Dominica comprises 10 administrative units known as parishes.

Parishes	Capitals
1. St. John	Portsmouth
2. St. Peter	Colihaut
3. St. Joseph	St. Joseph
4. St. Paul	Massacre
5. St. George	Roseau
6. St. Luke	Pointe Michael
7. St. Mark	Soufrière
8. St. Andrew	Marigot
9. St. David	Rosalie
10. St. Patrick	La Pleine

(1)   DOMINICAN REPUBLIC

(2)   Dominican Republic

(3)   República Dominicana

(4)   Dominican Republic is located in the eastern two-thirds of the Island of Santo Domingo, formerly Hispaniola, in the Caribbean.

(5)   Santo Domingo

(6)   Dominican Republic **comprises** 27 administrative units; 1 national capital district (Santo Domingo) and 26 provinces.

Provinces	Capitals
1. La Altagracia	Higüey
2. Azua	Azua de Compostella
3. Bahoruco	Neiba
4. Barahona	Santa Cruz de Barahona
5. Dajabón	Dajabón
6. Duarte	San Francisco de Marcorís
7. Espaillat	Moca
8. La Estrelleta	Elías Piña
9. Independencia	Jimaní
10. María Trinidad Sánchez	María Trinidad Sánchez
11. Montecristi	Montecristi
12. Pedernales	Pedernales
13. Peravia	Baní
14. Puerto Plata	Puerto Plata

15. La Romana	La Romana
16. Salcedo	Salcedo
17. Samaná	Samaná
18. San Cristóbal	San Cristóbal
19. San Juan	San Juan
20. San Pedro de Macorís	San Pedro de Macorís
21. Santiago	Santiago de los Caballeros
22. Santiago Rodríguez	Santiago Rodríguez
23. El Seibo	El Seibo
24. Valverde	Valverde
25. La Vega	La Vega
26. Sánchez Ramírez	Cotui

(1) EAST GERMANY

(2) German Democratic Republic

(3) Deutsche Demokratische Republik

(4) East Germany is located in eastern Europe. It is bounded by the **Baltic** Sea on the north; by Poland on the east; by Czechoslovakia and West Germany on the south; and by West Germany on the west.

(5) East Berlin

(6) East Germany comprises 15 administrative units known as districts.

Districts	Capitals
1. Berlin (East)	Berlin (East)
2. Cottbus	Cottbus
3. Dresden	Dresden
4. Erfurt	Erfurt
5. Frankfurt an der Oder	Frankfurt an der Oder
6. Gera	Gera
7. Halle an der Saale	Halle an der Saale
8. Karl-Marx-Stadt	Karl-Marx-Stadt
9. Leipzig	Leipzig
10. Magdeburg	Magdeburg
11. Neubrandenburg	Neubrandenburg
12. Potsdam	Potsdam
13. Rostock	Rostock
14. Schwerin	Schwerin
15. Suhl	Suhl

(1) EASTER ISLAND

(2) Easter Island, a Dependency of Chile

(3) Isla de Pascua

(4) Easter Island lies in the Pacific, west of Chile at a precise location of 27°3'-27°12' south latitude, 109°14'-109°28' west longitude.

(5) Hanga Roa

(6) Easter Island has but one settlement, the capital town of Hanga Roa. There are currently no divisions.

(1) ECUADOR

(2) Republic of Ecuador

(3) República del Ecuador

(4) Ecuador is bounded on the north by Colombia, on the east and south by Peru, and on the west by the Pacific Ocean.

(5) Quito

(6) Ecuador comprises 20 administrative units known as provinces.

Provinces		Capitals
1.	Azuay	Cuenca
2.	Bolívar	Guaranda
3.	Cañar	Azogues
4.	Carchi	Tulcán
5.	Cotopaxi	Latacunga
6.	Chimborazo	Riobamba
7.	El Oro	Machala
8.	Esmeraldes	Esmeraldes
9.	Guayas	Guayaquil
10.	Imbabura	Ibarra
11.	Loja	Loja
12.	Los Ríos	Babahoyo
13.	Manabí	Portoviejo
14.	Morona-Santiago	Macas
15.	Napo	Tena
16.	Pastazo	Puyo
17.	Pichincha	Quito
18.	Tungurahua	Ambato

19. Zamora-Chinchipe   Zamora
20. Archipiélago de Colón   Puerto Baquerizo

(1) EGYPT

(2) Arab Republic of Egypt

(3) Jumhuriyat Misr Al-^CArabiyah

(4) Egypt occupies the northeastern corner of Africa, with an ex-
     tension across the Gulf of Suez into the Sinai region, which
     is usually regarded as lying in Asia. It is bounded to the
     north by the Mediterranean, to the northeast by Israel, to
     the east by the Red Sea, to the south by Sudan, and to the
     west by Libya.

(5) Cairo

(6) Egypt comprises 25 administrative units known as governorates.

Governorates	Capitals
1. Cairo	Cairo
2. Alexandria	Alexandria
3. Suez	Suez
4. Port Said	Port Said
5. Ismailia	Ismailia
6. Damietta	Damietta
7. Behera	Damanhûr
8. Garbîya	Tanta
9. Daqahlîya	Mansûra
10. Sharqıya	Zagazig
11. Menûfîya	Shibin-el-Kôm
12. Qalyûbîya	Benha
13. Kafr el Sheikh	Kafr el Sheikh
14. Gıza	Gîza
15. Beni Suef	Beni Suef
16. Faiyûm	Faiyûm
17. Minya	Minya
18. Asyût	Asyût
19. Sohag	Sohag
20. Qena	Qena
21. Aswân	Aswân
22. Red Sea	Hurghada
23. New Valley	New Valley
24. Matrûh	Matrûh
25. Sinai	Sinai

(1) EL SALVADOR

(2) Republic of El Salvador

(3) República de El Salvador

(4) El Salvador lies on the Pacific coast of Central America. It is bounded by Guatemala to the west and Honduras to the north and east.

(5) San Salvador

(6) El Salvador comprises 14 administrative units known as departments.

Departments	Capitals
1. Ahuachapan	Ahuachapan
2. Cabañas	Sensuntepeque
3. Chalatenango	Chalatenango
4. Cuscatlán	Cojutepeque
5. La Libertad	Nueva San Salvador
6. La Paz	Zacatecoluca
7. La Union	La Union
8. Marazán	San Francisco Gotera
9. Santa Ana	Santa Ana
10. San Salvador	San Salvador
11. San Vicente	San Vicente
12. Sonsonate	Sonsonate
13. Usulatán	Usulatán
14. San Miguel	San Miguel

(1) EQUATORIAL GUINEA

(2) Republic of Equatorial Guinea

(3) República de Guinea Ecuatorial

(4) The country consists of two territories: the continental African province formerly called Rio Muni and the island formerly called Fernando Poo in the Gulf of Guinea.

(5) Malabo

(6) Equatorial Guinea comprises 2 administrative units known as provinces.

Provinces	Capitals
1. Bioko	Malabo
2. Rio Muni	Bata

(1) ETHIOPIA

(2) Socialist Republic of Ethiopia

(3) Itiopya

(4) Ethiopia is situated on the east side of Africa above the equator, lying between the White Nile and the Red Sea. It is bounded on the north and west by Sudan, on the east by the Red **Sea and Djibouti, on** the southeast by Somalia, and on the south by Kenya.

(5) Addis Ababa

(6) Ethiopia comprises 15 administrative units known as regions.

Regions	Capitals
1. Arussi	Assela
2. Bale	Goba
3. Begemdir	Gondar
4. Eritrea	Asmara
5. Gemu Goffa	Arba Minch
6. Gojjam	Debre Markos
7. **Hararge**	Harar
8. Illubabor	Mattu
9. Kefa	Jimma
10. Shoa	Addis Ababa
11. Sidamo	Awassa
12. Tigre	Mekele
13. Wollega	Lekemti
14. Wollo	Dessie
15. Addis Ababa	Addis Ababa

(1) FAEROE ISLANDS

(2) Faeroe Islands

(3) Faerøerne

(4) The Faeroes constitute a group of 18 inhabited islands in the

47

Atlantic Ocean, northwest of Scotland, with an area of some 540 square miles.

(5) Tórshavn

(6) Faroe Islands comprises 8 administrative units; 1 municipality or "bykommune" (Torshavn) and 7 districts or "syssel."

Syssel	Capitals
1. Norderoernes	Vidareidi
2. Osteroy	Eidi
3. Sandoy	Sandur
4. Stromoy	Tórshavn
5. Suderoy Nodre	Hvalbøur
6. Suderoy Sondre	Sumba
7. Vagar	Sørvagur

(1) FALKLAND ISLANDS

(2) Falkland Islands and Dependencies

(3) British Crown Colony of the Falkland Islands and Dependencies

(4) The Falklands are situated in the South Atlantic Ocean about 480 miles northeast of Cape Horn.

(5) Stanley

(6) Falkland Islands and dependencies comprise 3 administrative units known as districts.

Districts	Capitals
1. Stanley	Stanley
2. East Falkland	Stanley
3. West Falkland	Port Egmont

(1) FIJI

(2) Dominion of Fiji

(3) Dominion of Fiji

(4) Fiji consists of 844 islands located in the Pacific Ocean lying between 15° and 22° south latitude and 174° East and 177° west longitude.

(5)   Suva

(6)   Fiji comprises 18 administrative units; 4 divisions and 14
      provinces or "yasanas."

Divisions	Capitals
1. Northern	Lambasa
2. Eastern	Levuka
3. Western	Lautoka
4. Central	Nausori

Yasanas	Capitals
5. Nadroga/Navosa	Sigatoka
6. Ba	Lautoka
7. Ra	Rakiraki
8. Tailevu	Korovou
9. Naitasiri	Tamavua
10. Rewa	Lokia
11. Serua	Navua
12. Namosi	Mau
13. Bau	Bau
14. Macuata	Lambasa
15. Cakaudrove	Savusavu
16. Lau	Lau
17. Kadavu	Vanisea
18. Lomaniti	Levuka

(1)   FINLAND

(2)   Republic of Finland

(3)   Suomen Tasavalta

(4)   Finland is located in northern Europe. It is bounded by Nor-
      way on the north; by the U.S.S.R. on the east; by the Gulf
      of Finland, the U.S.S.R., and the Baltic Sea on the south;
      and by the Gulf of Bosnia, Sweden, and Norway on the west.

(5)   Helsinki

(6)   Finland comprises 12 administrative units known as provinces
      or "Läänit."

Läänit	Capitals
1. Lappi	Ravaniemi
2. Oulu	Oulu
3. Kuopio	Kuopio
4. Pohjois-Karjala	Joensusu

5. Keski-Suomen	Jwäskylä
6. Vaasa	Vaasa
7. Mikkeli	Mikkeli
8. Häme	Hämeenlinna
9. Turku-ja-Pori	Turku
10. Kymi	Kouvola
11. Uusimaa	Helsinki
12. Ahvenanmaa	Marianhamina

(1) FRANCE

(2) Republic of France

(3) République Française

(4) France is bounded in the north by the English Channel; in the
northeast by Belgium and Luxembourg; in the east by the
Federal Republic of Germany, Switzerland, and Italy; in the
south by the Mediterranean; in the southwest by Spain and
Andorra; and in the west by the Atlantic Ocean.

(5) Paris

(6) France comprises 118 administrative units; 22 régions or "circonscriptions d'action régionale" and 96 départements.

Régions	Capitals
1. Île-de-France	Paris
2. Champagne-Ardenne	Reims
3. Picardie	Amiens
4. Haute-Normandie	Rouen
5. Centre	Orleans
6. Basse-Normandie	Caen
7. Bourgogne	Dijon
8. Nord	Lille
9. Lorraine	Nancy
10. Alsace	Strasbourg
11. Franche-Comté	Besançon
12. Pays de la Loire	Nantes
13. Bretagne	Rennes
14. Poitou-Charentes	Poitiers
15. Aquitaine	**Bordeaux**
16. Midi-Pyrénées	Toulouse
17. Limousin	Limoges
18. Rhône-Alpes	Lyon
19. Auvergne	Clermont-Ferrand
20. Languedoc-Roussillon	Montpellier
21. Provence-Côte d'Azur	Marseille
22. Corse	Ajaccio

Départements	Capitals
23. Ain	Bourg-en-Bresse
24. Aisne	Laon
25. Allier	Moulins
26. Alpes-de-Haute-Provence	Digne
27. Alpes (Haute-)	Gap
28. Alpes-Maritimes	Nice
29. Ardèche	Privas
30. Ardennes	Charleville-Mézières
31. Ariège	Foix
32. Aube	Troyes
33. Aude	Carcassonne
34. Aveyron	Rodez
35. Belfort (Territoire de)	Belfort
36. Bouches-du-Rhône	Marseille
37. Calvados	Caen
38. Cantal	Aurillac
39. Charente	Angoulême
40. Charente-Maritime	La Rochelle
41. Cher	Bourges
42. Corrèze	Tulle
43. Corse-du-Sud	Ajaccio
44. Corse (Haute-)	Bastia
45. Côtes-du-Nord	St-Brieuc
46. Côte-d'Or	Dijon
47. Creuse	Guéret
48. Dordogne	Périgueux
49. Doubs	Besançon
50. Drôme	Valence
51. Essone	Évry
52. Eure	Évreux
53. Eure-et-Loir	Chartres
54. Finistère	Quimper
55. Gard	Nîmes
56. Garonne (Haute-)	Toulouse
57. Gers	Auch
58. Gironde	Bordeaux
59. Hauts-de-Seine	Nanterre
60. Hérault	Montpellier
61. Île-et-Vilaine	Rennes
62. Indre	Châteauroux
63. Indre-et-Loire	Tours
64. Isère	Grenoble
65. Jura	Lons-le-Saunier
66. Landes	Mont-de-Marsan
67. Loir-et-Cher	Blois
68. Loir	St.-Étienne
69. Loire (Haute-)	Le Puy
70. Loire-Atlantique	Nantes
71. Loiret	Orléans
72. Lot	Cahors
73. Lot-et-Garonne	Agen

74.	Lozère	Mende
75.	Maine-et-Loire	Angers
76.	Manche	Saint-Lô
77.	Marne	Châlons-sur-Marne
78.	Marne (Haute-)	Chaumont
79.	Mayenne	Laval
80.	Meurthe-et-Moselle	Nancy
81.	Meuse	Bar-le-Duc
82.	Morbihan	Vannes
83.	Moselle	Metz
84.	Nièvre	Nevers
85.	Nord	Lille
86.	Oise	Beauvais
87.	Orne	Alençon
88.	Paris (Ville de)	Paris
89.	Pas-de-Calais	Arras
90.	Puy-de-Dôme	Clermont-Ferrand
91.	Pyrénées-Atlantiques	Pau
92.	Pyrénées (Hautes-)	Tarbes
93.	**Pyrénées-Orientales**	Perpignan
94.	Rhin (Bas-)	Strasbourg
95.	Rhin (Haut-)	Colmar
96.	Rhône	Lyon
97.	Saône (Haute-)	Vesoul
98.	Saône-et-Loire	Mâcon
99.	Sarthe	Le Mans
100.	Savoie	Chambéry
101.	Savoie (Haute-)	Annecy
102.	Seine-Maritime	Rouen
103.	Seine-et-Marne	Melun
104.	Seine-Saint-Denis	Bobigny
105.	Sèvres (Deux-)	Niort
106.	Somme	Amiens
107.	Tarn	Albi
108.	Tarn-et-Garonne	Montauban
109.	Val-de-Marne	Créteil
110.	Val-d'Oise	Pontoise
111.	Var	Toulon
112.	Vaucluse	Avignon
113.	Vendée	La Roche-sur-Yon
114.	Vienne	Poitiers
115.	Vienne (Haute-)	Limoges
116.	Vosges	Épinal
117.	Yonne	Auxerre
118.	Yvelines	Versailles

(1)   FRENCH GUIANA

(2)   French Guiana Overseas Department

(3) La Guyane Française Département d'Outremer

(4) French Guiana is situated on the northeast coast of South America.

(5) Cayenne

(6) French Guiana comprises 23 administrative units; 2 arrondissements and 21 communes.

Arrondissements	Capitals
1. Cayenne	Cayenne
2. St. Laurent	St. Laurent-du-Maroni

Communes
3. Camopi
4. Cayenne
5. Iracoubo
6. Kourou
7. Macouria
8. Matoury
9. Montsinérv-Tonnégrande
10. Quanary
11. Régina
12. Remire-Montjoly
13. Roura
14. Saint-Elie
15. Saint-Georges
16. Sinnamary
17. Mana
18. Grand-Santi
19. Maripasoula
20. **Saül**
21. Saint-Laurent-du-Maroni
22. Papaîchton
23. Kaw

(1) FRENCH POLYNESIA

(2) French Polynesia Overseas Territory

(3) Polynésie Française Territoire Outremer

(4) French Polynesia consists of islands scattered over a wide area in the eastern Pacific Ocean, between 7° and 27° south latitude and 134° and 155° west longitude.

(5) Papeété, Island of Tahiti

(6) French Polynesia comprises 5 administrative units known as divisions or "circonscriptions."

Circonscriptions	Capitals
1. Îles du Vent	Papeété
2. Îles Sous le Vent	Utoroa (Raiatea I.)
3. Tuamotu et Gambier	Rangiroa
4. Îles Australes	Mataura (Tubuai I.)
5. Îles Marquises	Hakapehi (Nuku Hiva Island)

(1) FRENCH SOUTHERN AND ANTARCTIC LANDS

(2) French Southern and Antarctic Lands

(3) Terres Australes et Antarctiques Françaises

(4) T.A.A.F. is an administrative framework of a group of islands at the southern extremity of the Indian Ocean including the French portion of the Antarctic continent.

(5) Port-aux-Français

(6) The French Southern and Antarctic Lands have only a scientific outpost with extremely few inhabitants, and no requirement for administrative divisions.

(1) GABON

(2) The Gabon Republic

(3) République Gabonaise

(4) Gabon is bounded on the west by the Atlantic Ocean, on the north by Equatorial Guinea and Cameroon, and on the east and south by Congo.

(5) Libreville

(6) Gabon comprises 45 administrative units; 9 provinces or "régions" and 36 districts or "sous-préfectures."

Régions	Capitals
1. Estuaire	Libreville
2. Haut-Ogooué	Franceville
3. Moyen-Ogooué	Lambaréné

4. Ngounié	Mouila
5. Ogooué-Ivindo	Makokou
6. Nyanga	Tchibanga
7. Ogooué-Lolo	Koulamoutou
8. Ogooué-Marîtime	Port Gentil
9. Woleu-Ntem	Oyem

Sous-Préfectures	Capitals
10. Libreville	Libreville
11. Owendo	Owendo
12. N'Toum	N'Toum
13. Cocobeach	Cocobeach
14. M'Foulenzem	M'Foulenzem
15. Kango	Kango
16. Port Gentil	Port Gentil
17. Omboué	Omboué
18. Tchibanga	Tchibanga
19. Mayumba	Mayumba
20. Moabi	Moabi
21. Lambaréné	Lambaréné
22. N'Djole	N'Djole
23. Mouila	Mouila
24. Mandji	Mandji
25. Fougamou	Fougamou
26. Sindara	Sindara
27. Lébamba	Lébamba
28. Ndendé	Ndendé
29. Mbigou	Mbigou
30. Mimongo	Mimongo
31. Oyem	Oyem
32. Mitzic	Mitzic
33. Médouneu	Médouneu
34. Bitam	Bitam
35. Minvoul	Minvoul
36. Makoukou	Makoukou
37. Booué	Booué
38. Mékambo	Mékambo
39. Koulamoutou	Koulamoutou
40. Lastourville	Lastourville
41. Franceville	Franceville
42. Moanda	Moanda
43. Bakoumba	Bakoumba
44. Leconi	Leconi
45. Okondja	Okondja

(1) GAMBIA

(2) The Republic of the Gambia

(3)   The Republic of the Gambia

(4)   Gambia is bounded in the west by the Atlantic Ocean and on
      all other sides by Senegal.

(5)   Banjul

(6)   Gambia comprises 6 administrative units; 1 federal capital dis-
      trict (Banjul) and 5 area councils.

Area Councils	Capitals
1. Western	Brikama
2. Central	Mansa Konko
3. MacCarthy	Georgetown
4. Upper River	Basse
5. Kerewan	Kerewan

(1)   GHANA

(2)   State of Ghana

(3)   State of Ghana

(4)   Ghana (formerly the Gold Coast) lies on the west coast of
      Africa between 1°12' east and 3°15' west longitude and 11°11'
      north latitude. It is bounded on the south by Gulf of Guinea,
      on the east by Togo, on the north by Haut Volta, and on the
      west by Ivory Coast.

(5)   Accra

(6)   Ghana comrpises 9 administrative units known as regions.

Regions	Capitals
1. Western	Sekondi-Takoradi
2. Central	Cape Coast
3. Greater Accra	Accra
4. Eastern	Koforidua
5. Volta	Ho
6. Ashanti	Kumasi
7. Brong-Ahafo	Sunyani
8. Northern	Tamale
9. Upper	Bolgatanga

(2)   Crown Colony of Gibraltar

(3)   Crown Colony of Gibraltar

(4)   Gibraltar is a rocky promontory near the southern extremity
       of Spain, with which it is connected by a low isthmus.   It is
       two and three-quarters miles in length by three-quarters of
       a mile in breadth and has a total area of two and one-quarter
       square miles.

(5)   Gibraltar City

(6)   Gibraltar comprises 5 administrative units known as districts.

Districts
1.   The City
2.   South District
3.   North Front
4.   The Port
5.   Upper Rock

(1)   GREECE

(2)   Democratic Republic of Greece

(3)   Elliniki Dimokratia

(4)   Greece is bounded on the north by Albania, Yugoslavia, and
       Bulgaria; on the east by Turkey and the Aegean Sea; on the
       south by the Mediterranean Sea; and on the west by the
       Ionian Sea.

(5)   Athens

(6)   Greece comprises 54 administrative units; 1 national capital
       district (Athens), 1 autonomous prefecture (Mt. Athos/Karyi,
       capital) and 52 prefectures or "nomoi."

Nomoi	Capitals
1. Aetolia and Acarnania	Missolonghi
2. Attica	Athens
3. Boeotia	Levadeia
4. Euboea	Chalcis
5. Evrytania	Karpenissi
6. Phthiotis	Lamia

7.	Phokis	Amphissa
8.	Piraeus	Piraeus
9.	Argolis	Nauplion
10.	Arcadia	Tripolis
11.	Akhaïa	Patras
12.	Elia	Pyrgos
13.	Korinthia	Korinthos
14.	Lakonia	Sparte
15.	Messenia	Calamata
16.	Zakynthos	Zante
17.	Kerkyra	Kerkyra
18.	Kefallenia	Argostolion
19.	Lefkas	Lefkas
20.	Arta	Arta
21.	Thesprotia	Hegoumenitsa
22.	Yannina	Yannina
23.	Preveza	Preveza
24.	Karditsa	Karditsa
25.	Larissa	Larissa
26.	Magnessia	Volos
27.	Trikkala	Trikkala
28.	Grevena	Grevena
29.	Drama	Drama
30.	Imathia	Verria
31.	Thessaloniki	Thessaloniki
32.	Kavala	Kavala
33.	Kastoria	Kastoria
34.	Kilkis	Kilkis
35.	Kozani	Kozani
36.	Pella	Edessa
37.	Pieria	Katerini
38.	Serres	Serres
39.	Florina	Florina
40.	Khalkidiki	Polyghyros
41.	Evros	Alexandroupolis
42.	Xanthi	Xanthi
43.	Rodopi	Komotini
44.	Cyclades	Hermoupolis
45.	Lesvos	Mitylini
46.	Samos	Limin Vatheos
47.	Khios	Khios
48.	Dodecanese	Rhodes
49.	Iraklion	Heraklion
50.	Lassithi	Aghios Nikolaos
51.	Rethymnon	Rethymnon
52.	Canea	Canea

(1) GREENLAND

(2) Greenland

(3) Grønland

(4) Greenland covers an area of over two million square kilometers, the world's largest island. The country stretches from the Arctic Ocean as far south as Oslo latitude.

(5) Nûk (Godthåb)

(6) Greenland comprises 22 administrative units; 19 municipalities or "byer" and 3 subprovinces or "landsdele."

Byer
1. Angmagssalik
2. Christianshåb
3. Egedesminde
4. Frederikshåb
5. Godhavn
6. Godthåb
7. Holsteinsborg
8. Ivigtut
9. Jakobshavn
10. Julianehåb
11. Kangalsiaq
12. Nanortalik
13. Narssaq
14. Scorebysand
15. Sukkertoppen
16. Thule
17. Umanak
18. Upernavik
19. Vaigat

Landsdele	Capitals
20. West Greenland	Godthåb
21. East Greenland	Angmagssalik
22. North Greenland	Thule

(1) GRENADA

(2) The State of Grenada

(3) The State of Grenada

59

(4) Grenada is the most southerly island in the Caribbean group known as The Windward Islands.

(5) St. George's

(6) Grenada comprises 6 administrative units known as parishes.

Parishes	Capitals
1. St. David	St. David's
2. St. George	St. George's
3. St. John	Gouyave
4. St. Mark	Victoria
5. St. Patrick	Sauteurs
6. St. Andrew	Grenville

(1) GUADELOUPE

(2) French Overseas Department of Guadeloupe

(3) **Guadeloupe Département Outremer**

(4) Guadeloupe consists of a group of islands in the Caribbean's Lesser Antilles, between latitude north 15°52' and 18°07', and 61°03' and 63°05' longitude west.

(5) Basse-Terre

(6) Guadeloupe comprises 37 administrative units; 3 districts or "arrondissements" and 34 subdivisions or "cantons."

Arrondissements	Capitals
1. Basse-Terre	Basse-Terre
2. Pointe-à-Pitre	Pointe-à-Pitre
3. St. Barthelemy-St. Martin	St. Barthelemy

Cantons	Capitals
4. Les Abymes	Les Abymes
5. Anse-Bertrand	Anse-Bertrand
6. Baie-Mahault	Baie-Mahault
7. Baillif	Baillif
8. Basse-Terre	Basse-Terre
9. Bouillante	Bouillante
10. Capesterre-de-Guadeloupe	Capesterre-de-Guadeloupe
11. Capesterre-de-Marie-Galante	Capesterre-de-Marie-Galante
12. Gourbeyre	Gourbeyre
13. La Desirade	La Desirade
14. Deshaies	Deshaies
15. Lamentin	Lamentin

16.	Morne-a-l'Eau	Morne-a-l'Eau
17.	Le Moule	Le Moule
18.	Petit-Bourg	Petit-Bourg
19.	Petit-Canal	Petit-Canal
20.	Pointe-a-Pitre	Pointe-a-Pitre
21.	Pointe-Noire	Pointe-Noire
22.	Grand-Bourg	Grand-Bourg
23.	Le Gosier	Le Gosier
24.	Goyave	Goyave
25.	Port-Louis	Port-Louis
26.	Saint-Barthelemy	Saint-Barthelemy
27.	Saint-Claude	**Saint-Claude**
28.	Saint-François	Saint-François
29.	Saint-Louis	Saint-Louis
30.	Saint-Martin	Saint-Martin
31.	Sainte-Anne	Sainte-Anne
32.	Sainte-Rose	Sainte-Rose
33.	Terre-de-Bas	Terre-de-Bas
34.	Terre-de-Haut	Terre-de-Haut
35.	Trois-Rivieres	Trois-Rivieres
36.	Vieux-Fort	Vieux-Fort
37.	Vieux-Habitants	Vieux-Habitants

(1) GUAM

(2) Guam, a U.S. Unincorporated Territory

(3) Guam, a U.S. Unincorporated Territory

(4) Guam is the largest and most southern island of the Marianas Archipelago, in 13°26' north latitude, 144°43' east longitude.

(5) Agaña

(6) Guam comprises 15 administrative units known as municipalities.

<u>Municipalities</u>
1. Agaña
2. Agat
3. Asan
4. Barrigada
5. Dededo
6. Inarajan
7. Machanao
8. Merizo
9. Piti
10. Sinaiana
11. Sumay

12. Talofof
13. Umatac
14. Yigo
15. Yona

(1) GUATEMALA

(2) Republic of Guatemala

(3) República de Guatemala

(4) Guatemala is bounded on the north and on the west by Mexico, on the south by the Pacific Ocean, and on the east by El Salvador.

(5) Guatemala City

(6) Guatemala comprises 22 administrative units known as departments.

Departments	Capitals
1. Alta Verapaz	Cobán
2. Baja Verapaz	Salamá
3. Chimaltenango	Chimaltenango
4. Chiquimula	Chiquimula
5. El Progreso	El Progreso
6. Escuintla	Escuintla
7. Guatemala	Guatemala City
8. Huehuetenango	Huehuetenango
9. Izabal	Puerto Barrios
10. Jalapa	Jalapa
11. Jutiapa	Jutiapa
12. Peten	Flores
13. Quezaltenango	Quezaltenango
14. Quiche	Santa Cruz del Quiche
15. Retalhuleu	Retalhuleu
16. Sacatepequez	Antique Guatemala
17. San Marcos	San Marcos
18. Santa Rosa	Cuilapa
19. Sololá	Sololá
20. Suchitepéquez	Mazatenango
21. Totonicapán	Totonicapán
22. Zacapa	Zacapa

(1) GUINEA

(2) Republic of Guinea

(3) République de Guinée

(4) Guinea is bounded on the northwest by Guinea-Bissau and on the south by Liberia and Sierra Leone.

(5) Conakry

(6) Guinea comprises 31 administrative units; 4 "supra-régions" and 27 "régions."

Supra-Régions	Capitals
1. Guinée-Maritime	Kindia
2. Moyenne-Guinée	Labé
3. Haute-Guinée	Kankan
4. Guinée-Forestière	N'Zérékoré

Regions	Capitals
5. Beyla	Beyla
6. Boffa	Boffa
7. Boké	Boké
8. Conakry	Conakry
9. Dalaba	Dalaba
10. Dinguiraye	Dinguiraye
11. Dubréka	Dubréka
12. Faranah	Faranah
13. Forécariah	Forécariah
14. Fria	Fria
15. Guéckédou	Guéckédou
16. Kankan	Kankan
17. Kindia	Kindia
18. Kissidougou	Kissidougou
19. Kouroussa	Kouroussa
20. Labé	Labé
21. Macenta	Macenta
22. Mali	Mali
23. Mamou	Mamou
24. N'Zérékoré	N'Zérékoré
25. Pita	Pita
26. Siguiri	Siguiri
27. Télimélé	Télimélé
28. Tongué	Tongué
29. Youkounkoun	Youkounkoun
30. Gaoual	Gaoual
31. Dabola	Dabola

(1) GUINEA-BISSAU

(2) The Republic of Guinea-Bissau

(3) República Guiné-Bissau

(4) Guinea-Bissau is bounded by Senegal in the north, and by Guinea in the east and south.

(5) Bissau

(6) Guinea-Bissau comprises 9 administrative units known as regions or "região."

Região	Capitals
1. Bissau	Bissau
2. Bafatá	Bafatá
3. Biombo	Biombo
4. Bolama-Bijagos	Bolama-Bijagos
5. Buba	Buba
6. Cacheu	Cacheu
7. Gabú	Gabú Sara
8. Oio	Farim
9. Tombali	Catió

(1) GUYANA

(2) Cooperative Republic of Guyana

(3) Cooperative Republic of Guyana

(4) Guyana is situated on the northeast coast of South America on the Atlantic Ocean, with Surinam on the east, Venezuela on the west, and Brazil on the south and west.

(5) Georgetown

(6) Guyana comprises 9 administrative units known as districts.

Districts	Capitals
1. East Berbice	New Amsterdam
2. West Berbice	Fort Wellington
3. East Demerara	Emmore
4. West Demerara	Vreed en Hoop
5. Essequibo	Suddie
6. Essequibo Islands	Enterprise
7. North-West	Mabaruma

8. Mazaruni-Potaro	Bartica
9. Rupununi	Letham

(1) HAITI

(2) Republic of Haiti

(3) République d'Haiti

(4) Haiti occupies the western third of the large Caribbean island of Hispaniola. Its neighbor on this island is the Dominican Republic.

(5) Port-au-Prince

(6) Haiti comprises 9 administrative units known as départements.

Départements	Capitals
1. Nord	Cap-Haitien
2. Nord-Ouest	Port-de-Paix
3. Nord-Est	Fort Liberté
4. Artibonite	Gonaives
5. Centre	Hinche
6. Sud Est	Jacmel
7. Grand Anse	Jeremie
8. Sud	Les Cayes
9. Ouest	Port-au-Prince

(1) HONDURAS

(2) Republic of Honduras

(3) República de Honduras

(4) Honduras is bounded on the north by the Caribbean, on the east and northeast by Nicaragua, on the west by Guatemala, on the southwest by El Salvador, and on the south by the Pacific Ocean.

(5) Tegucigalpa

(6) Honduras comprises 18 administrative units known as departments.

Departments	Capitals
1. Francisco Morazán	Tegucigalpa

2.	Atlantida	La Ceiba
3.	Colon	Trujillo
4.	Comayagua	Comayagua
5.	Copán	Santa Rosa de Copán
6.	Cortés	San Pedro Sula
7.	Choluteca	Choluteca
8.	El Paráiso	Yuscarán
9.	Gracias a Dios	Gracias a Dios
10.	Intibucá	La Esperanza
11.	Islas de la Bahia	Roatán
12.	La Paz	La Paz
13.	Lempira	Graciás
14.	Ocotepeque	Nueva Ocotepeque
15.	Olancho	Juticalpa
16.	Santa Bárbara	Santa Bárbara
17.	Valle	Nacoame
18.	**Yoro**	**Yoro**

(1) HONG KONG

(2) Crown Colony of Hong Kong

(3) Crown Colony of Hong Kong

(4) Hong Kong Island is 20 miles east of the mouth of China's Pearl River and 91 miles southeast of Canton. The colony also encompasses Kowloon and its environs called "The New Territories."

(5) Victoria

(6) Hong Kong comprises 18 administrative units known as districts.

Districts		Capitals
1.	North	Shek Wu Hui
2.	Yuen Long	Yuen Long
3.	Tai Po	Tai Po
4.	Tuen Mun	Tuen Mun
5.	Sha Tin	Sha Tin
6.	Tsuen Wan	Tsuen Wan
7.	Sai Kung	Sai Kung
8.	Islands	Lantau Island
9.	**Central and Western**	Victoria
10.	Wan Chai	Wan Chai
11.	Southern	Stanley
12.	Yau Ma Tei	Yau Ma Tei
13.	Mong Kok	Mong Kok
14.	Sham Shui Po	Sham Shui Po

15.	Kowloon City	Kowloon City
16.	Kwun Tong	Kwun Tong
17.	Wong Tai Sin	Wong Tai Sin
18.	Eastern	Mt. Collinson

(1) HUNGARY

(2) People's Republic of Hungary

(3) Magyar Népköztársaság

(4) Hungary is bounded on the north by Czechoslovakia, on the northeast by the U.S.S.R., on the east by Romania, on the south by Yugoslavia, and on the west by Austria.

(5) Budapest

(6) Hungary comprises 25 administrative units; 6 county boroughs and 19 counties or "megye."

County Boroughs
1. Budapest
2. Debrecen
3. Györ
4. Miskolc
5. Pécs
6. Szeged

Megye	Capitals
7. Baranya	Pécs
8. Bács-Kiskun	Kecskemét
9. Békés	Békéscsaba
10. Borsod-Abaúj-Zemplén	Miskolc
11. Csongrád	Szeged
12. Fejér	Székesfehérvár
13. Györ-Sopron	Györ
14. Hajdú-Bihar	Derecen
15. Heves	Eger
16. Komárom	Tatabánya
17. Nógrád	Salgótarján
18. Pest	Budapest
19. Somogy	Kaposvár
20. Szabolcs-Szatmár	Nyíregyháza
21. Szolnok	Szolnok
22. Tolna	Szekszárd
23. Vas	Szombathely
24. Veszprém	Veszprém
25. Zala	Zalaegerszeg

(1) ICELAND

(2) Republic of Iceland

(3) Lýðveldið Island

(4) Iceland is a large island in the North Atlantic close to the Arctic Circle.

(5) Reykjavik

(6) Iceland comprises 37 administrative units; 23 counties or "sýslur" and 14 independent towns or "kaupstadhir."

Sýslur	Capitals
1. Arnessýsla	Selfoss
2. Austur-Bardhastrandarsýsla	Patreksfjordur
3. Austur-Húnavatnssýsla	Blönduós
4. Austur-Skaftafellssýsla	Vik i Mýrdal
5. Borgarfjardharsýsla	Borgarnes
6. Dalasýsla	Búdardalur
7. Eyjafjardsýsla	Eyjafjaroar
8. Gullbringusýsla	Gullbringu
9. Kjósardsýsla	Kjósur
10. Mýrasýsla	Borgarnes
11. Nordhur-Isafjardharsýsla	Isafjaroar
12. Nordhur-Múlasýsla	Múla
13. Nordur-Thingeyjarsýsla	Thingeyjar
14. Rangárvallasýsla	Hvolsvöllur
15. Skagafjardharsýsla	Skagafjaroar
16. Snaefellsnessýsla	Stykkisholmur
17. Strandasýsla	Hólmavík
18. Sudhur-Múlasýsla	Eskifjördur
19. Sudhur-Thingeyjarsýsla	Thingeyjar
20. Vestur-Bardhastrandarsýsla	Patreksfjórdur
21. Vestur-Húnavatnssýsla	Blönduós
22. Vestur-Ísafjardharsýsla	Isafjaroar
23. Vestur-Skaftafellssýsla	Vik i Mýrdal

Kaupstadhir
24. Arkranes
25. Akureyra
26. Hafnarfjördhur
27. Húsavík
28. Ísafjördhur
29. Keflavík
30. Kópavogur
31. Neskaupstadhur
32. Ólafsfjördur
33. Reykjavik

34. Saudhárkrókur
35. Seydhisfjördur
36. Siglufjördhur
37. Vestmannaeyjar

(1)   INDIA

(2)   Republic of India

(3)   Bharat

(4)   India is bounded on the northwest by Pakistan; on the north
      by China, Tibet, Nepal, and Bhutan; on the east by Burma;
      and on the southeast, south, and southwest by the Indian
      Ocean.

(5)   New Delhi

(6)   India comprises 31 administrative units; 9 union territories
      and 22 states.

Union Territories	Capitals
1. Chandigarh	Chandigarh
2. Andaman And Nicobar Islands	Port Blair
3. Arunachal Pradesh	Itanagar
4. Dadra And Nagar Haveli	Silvassa
5. Delhi	Delhi
6. Goa, Daman, And Diu	Panaji
7. Lakshadweep	Kavaratti
8. Mizoram	Aizawl
9. Pondicherry	Pondicherry

States	Capitals
10. Andhra Pradesh	Hyderabad
11. Assam	Dispur
12. Bihar	Patna
13. Gujarat	Gandhinager
14. Haryana	Chandigarh
15. Jammu And Kashmir	Srinagar
16. Karnataka	Bangalore
17. Kerala	Trivandrum
18. Madhya Pradesh	Bhopal
19. Maharashtra	Bombay
20. Manipur	Imphal
21. Meghalya	Shillong
22. Nagaland	Kohima
23. Orissa	Bhubaneswar

24.	Punjab	Chandigarh
25.	Rajasthan	Jaipur
26.	Sikkim	Gangtok
27.	Tamil Nadu	Madras
28.	Uttar Pradesh	Lucknow
29.	West Bengal	Calcutta
30.	Himachal Pradesh	Simla
31.	Tripura	Agartala

(1) INDONESIA

(2) Republic of Indonesia

(3) Republik Indonesia

(4) Indonesia comprises the former East Indies consisting of the islands of Java, Sumatra, Kalimantan, Sulawesi, and western New Guinea.

(5) Jakarta

(6) Indonesia comprises 27 administrative units known as provinces or "propinsi."

Propinsi		Capitals
1.	Aceh	Banda Aceh
2.	Sumatera Utara	Medan
3.	Sumatera Barat	Padang
4.	Riau	Pakanbaru
5.	Jambi	Telanaipura
6.	Sumatera Selatan	Palembang
7.	Bengkalu	Bengkalu
8.	Lampung	Tanjungkarang
9.	Jakarta Raya	Jakarta
10.	Jawa Barat	Bandung
11.	Jawa Tengah	Semarang
12.	Yogyakarta	Yogyakarta
13.	Jawa Timur	Surabaya
14.	Kalimantan Barat	Pontianak
15.	Kalimantan Tengah	Palangkaraya
16.	Kalimantan Selatan	Banjarmasin
17.	Kalimantan Timur	Samarinda
18.	Sulawesi Utara	Menado
19.	Sulawesi Tengah	Palu
20.	Sulawesi Selatan	Ujung Padang
21.	Sulawesi Tenggara	Kendari
22.	Bali	Denpasar
23.	Nusu Tenggara Barat	Mataram

24.	Nusu Tenggara Timur	Kupang
25.	Loro Sae	Dili
26.	Maluku	Ambon
27.	Irian Jaya	Jajapura

(1)   IRAN

(2)   The Islamic Republic of Iran

(3)   Keshvaré Shahanshahivé

(4)   Iran is bounded on the north by the U.S.S.R. and the Caspian Sea, on the east by Afghanistan and Pakistan, on the south by the Persian Gulf and the Gulf of Oman, and on the west by Iraq and Turkey.

(5)   Tehran

(6)   Iran comprises 23 administrative units; 2 districts or "shahrestan," 6 governorates or "farmandari-ye koll" and 15 provinces or "ostan."

Shahrestan	Capitals
1. Yazd	Yazd
2. Zanjan	Zanjan

Farmandari-ye Koll	Capitals
3. Bakhtiyari Va Chaharmahal	Shahrekord
4. Boyerahmadi Va Kohkiluyeh	Yasuj
5. Hamadan	Hamadan
6. Ilam	Ilam
7. Lorestan	Khorramabad
8. Semnan	Semnan

Ostan	Capitals
9. Baluchestan Va Sistan	Zahedan
10. Bushehr	Bushehr
11. Markazi	Tehran
12. East Azerbaijan	Tabriz
13. West Azerbaijan	Rezayeh
14. Esfahan	Esfahan
15. Fars	Shiraz
16. Gilan	Rasht
17. Kerman	Kerman
18. Kermanshah	Kermanshah
19. Khuzistan	Ahwaz
20. Khorasan	Meshed
21. Kurdestan	Sanandaj

| 22. | Mazandaran | Sari |
| 23. | Hormozdgan | Bandar Abbas |

(1) IRAQ

(2) Republic of Iraq

(3) Al Jumhouriya al ^{C}Iraqia

(4) Iraq is bounded on the north by Turkey, on the east by Iran, on the southeast by the Persian Gulf, on the south by Saudi Arabia, and on the west by Jordan and Syria.

(5) Baghdad

(6) Iraq comprises 19 administrative units; 1 neutral zone (known as Neutral Zone/Baghdad, capital), 3 autonomous governorates and 15 governorates.

Autonomous Governorates	Capitals
1. Arbeel	Arbeel
2. Duhook	Duhook
3. Sulaimaniya	Sulaimaniya

Governorates	Capitals
4. Misaan	Amaara
5. Baghdad	Baghdad
6. Basrah	Basrah
7. Diyaala	Baqooba
8. Qadisiya	Diwaaniya
9. Babylon	Hilla
10. Waasit	Kut
11. Ninevah	Musil
12. Thee Qaar	Naasiriya
13. Anbaar	Ramaadi
14. Muthannaa	Simaawa
15. Tameem	Karkuk
16. Karbalaa	Karbalaa
17. Najaf	Najaf
18. Salaah Eddeen	Tikreet

(1) IRELAND

(2) Irish Republic

(3) Éire

72

(4) Ireland lies in the Atlantic Ocean, separated from Great Britain by the Irish Sea to the east, and bounded on the northeast by Northern Ireland.

(5) Dublin

(6) Ireland comprises 32 administrative units; 5 county boroughs and 27 counties.

County Boroughs
1. Dublin
2. Dun Laoghaire
3. Cork
4. Limerick
5. Waterford

Counties	Capitals
6. Carlow	Carlow
7. Dublin	Dublin
8. Kildaire	Naas
9. Kilkenny	Kilkenny
10. Laoighis	Port Laoighis
11. Longford	Longford
12. Louth	Dundalk
13. Meath	Navan
14. Offaly	Tullamore
15. Westmeath	Mullingar
16. Wexford	Wexford
17. Wicklow	Wicklow
18. Clare	Ennis
19. Cork	Cork
20. Kerry	Tralee
21. Limerick	Limerick
22. Tipperary, North Riding	Nenagh
23. Tipperary, South Riding	Clonmel
24. Waterford	Waterford
25. Galway	Galway
26. Leitrim	Carrick-On-Shannon
27. Mayo	Castlebar
28. Roscommon	Roscommon
29. Sligo	Sligo
30. Cavan	Cavan
31. Donegal	Lifford
32. Monaghan	Monaghan

(1) ISLE OF MAN

(2) Isle of Man

(3) Isle of Man

(4) The Isle of Man is situated in the Irish Sea, in latitude 54°3'
     north to 54°25' north and longitude 4°18' west to 4°47' west,
     nearly equidistant from England, Scotland, and Ireland.

(5) Douglas

(6) Isle of Man comprises 17 administrative units known as parishes
     or "paroisses."

Paroisses
1. Andreas
2. Arbory
3. Braddan
4. Bride
5. German
6. Jurby
7. Lezayre
8. Lonan
9. Malew
10. Maroun
11. Maughold
12. Michael
13. Onchan
14. Patrick
15. Rushen
16. Ballaugh
17. Santon

(1) ISRAEL

(2) State of Israel

(3) Medinat Israel

(4) The State of Israel lies at the eastern end of the Mediterranean
     Sea. It is bounded on the west by Egypt, on the east by
     Jordan, on the north by Lebanon, and on the northeast by
     Syria.

(5) Jerusalem

(6) Israel comprises 34 administrative units; 6 districts or "mehoz,"
     14 subdistricts or "nefa," 3 administered territories and 11
     administered territories subdistricts.

Mehoz	Capitals
1. Northern	Nazareth

2.	Haifa	Haifa
3.	Central	Ramla
4.	Tel Aviv	Tel Aviv
5.	Jerusalem	Jerusalem
6.	Southern	Beersheba

Nefa		Capitals
7.	Akko	Akko
8.	Ashqelon	Ashqelon
9.	Be'er Sheva	Be'er Sheva
10.	Hadera	Hadera
11.	Haifa	Haifa
12.	Jerusalem	Jerusalem
13.	Kinneret	Tiberias
14.	Petah-Tiqwa	Petah-Tiqwa
15.	Ramla	Ramla
16.	Rehovat	Rehovat
17.	Tel Aviv	Tel Aviv
18.	Yizre'el	Afula
19.	Zefat	Zefat
20.	Sharon	Netanya

Administered Territories		Capitals
21.	Judea and Samaria	Hebron
22.	Gaza Strip	Gaza
23.	Golan Heights	Quineitra

Administered Territories		
Subdistricts		Capitals
24.	Jenin	Jenin
25.	Nablus	Nablus
26.	Tulkarm	Tulkarm
27.	Ramallah	Ramallah
28.	Jericho	Jericho
29.	Bethlehem	Bethlehem
30.	Hebron	Hebron
31.	Gaza	Gaza
32.	Khan Yunis	Khan Yunis
33.	Sharm Esh-Sheikh	Sharm Esh-Sheikh
34.	Rafah	Rafah

(1) ITALY

(2) The Italian Republic

(3) Repubblica Italiana

(4) Italy is located in southern Europe, comprising a boot-shaped
peninsula extended into the Mediterranean. It is bounded by

Yugoslavia, the Adriatic Sea, and the Ionian Sea on the east, by the Tyrrhenian Sea on the south and the southwest; by the Ligurian Sea and France on the west; and by Switzerland on the north.

(5) Rome

(6) Italy comprises 114 administrative units; 20 regions and 94 provinces.

Regions	Capitals
1. Abruzzi	L'Aquila
2. Basilicata	Potenza
3. Calabria	Catanzaro
4. Campania	Naples
5. Emilia-Romagna	Bologna
6. Friuli-Venezia-Giulia	Trieste
7. Lazio	Rome
8. Liguria	Genoa
9. Lombardia	Milan
10. Marche	Ancona
11. Molise	Campobasso
12. Piemonte	Turin
13. Puglia	Bari
14. Sardegna	Cagliari
15. Sicilia	Palermo
16. Toscana	Florence
17. Trentino-Alto Adige	Bolzano and Trento
18. Umbria	Perugia
19. Valle d'Aosta	Aosta
20. Veneto	Venice

Provinces	Capitals
21. Bolzano	Bolzano
22. Trento	Trento
23. Arezzo	Arezzo
24. Firenze	Firenze
25. Grosseto	Grosseto
26. Livorno	Livorno
27. Lucca	Lucca
28. Massa-Carrara	Massa
29. Pisa	Pisa
30. Pistoria	Pistoria
31. Siena	Siena
32. Perugia	Perugia
33. Terni	Terni
34. Aosta	Aosta
35. Belluno	Belluno
36. Padova	Padua
37. Rovigo	Rovigo
38. Treviso	Treviso

39.	Venezia	Venezia
40.	Verona	Verona
41.	Vicenza	Vicenza
42.	Aquila	Aquila
43.	Chieti	Chieti
44.	Pescara	Pescara
45.	Teramo	Teramo
46.	Bari	Bari
47.	Brindisi	Brindisi
48.	Foggia	Foggia
49.	Lecca	Lecca
50.	Taranto	Taranto
51.	Matera	Matera
52.	Potenza	Potenza
53.	Catanzaro	Catanzaro
54.	Cosenza	Cosenza
55.	Reggio di Calabria	Reggio di Calabria
56.	Avellino	Avellino
57.	Benevento	Benevento
58.	Caserta	Caserta
59.	Napoli	Napoli
60.	Salerno	Salerno
61.	Bologna	Bologna
62.	Ferrara	Ferrara
63.	Forli	Forli
64.	Modena	Modena
65.	Parma	Parma
66.	Piacenza	Piacenza
67.	Ravenna	Ravenna
68.	Reggio nell'Emilia	Reggio nell'Emilia
69.	Gorizia	Gorizia
70.	Pordenone	Pordenone
71.	Trieste	Trieste
72.	Udine	Udine
73.	Frosinone	Frosinone
74.	Latina	Latina
75.	Rieti	Rieti
76.	Roma	Roma
77.	Viterbo	Viterbo
78.	Genova	Genova
79.	Imperia	Imperia
80.	La Spezia	La Spezia
81.	Savona	Savona
82.	Bergamo	Bergamo
83.	Brescia	Brescia
84.	Como	Como
85.	Cremona	Cremona
86.	Mantova	Mantova
87.	Milano	Milano
88.	Pavia	Pavia
89.	Sondrio	Sondrio

90.	Varese	Varese
91.	Ancona	Ancona
92.	Ascoli Piceno	Ascoli Piceno
93.	Macerata	Macerata
94.	Pesaro e Urbino	Pesaro
95.	Campobasso	Campobasso
96.	Isérnia	Isérnia
97.	Alessandria	Alessandria
98.	Asti	Asti
99.	Cuneo	Cuneo
100.	Novara	Novara
101.	Torino	Torino
102.	Vercelli	Vercelli
103.	Cagliari	Cagliari
104.	Nuoro	Nuoro
105.	Sassari	Sassari
106.	Agrigento	Agrigento
107.	Caltanisetta	Caltanisetta
108.	Catania	Catania
109.	Enna	Enna
110.	Messina	Messina
111.	Palermo	Palermo
112.	Ragusa	Ragusa
113.	Siracusa	Siracusa
114.	Trapani	Trapani

(1)   IVORY COAST

(2)   Republic of the Ivory Coast

(3)   République de Côte d'Ivoire

(4)   Ivory Coast is situated between Liberia and Ghana and has
        common frontiers with the Republics of Guinea, Mali, and
        Upper Volta.

(5)   Abidjan

(6)   Ivory Coast comprises 26 administrative units known as depart-
        ments.

Departments		Capitals
1.	Abengourou	Abengourou
2.	Abidjan	Abidjan
3.	Aboisso	Aboisso
4.	Adzopé	Adzopé
5.	Agboville	Agboville
6.	Biankouma	Biankouma

7.	Bondoukou	Bondoukou
8.	Bouaké	Bouaké
9.	Bouna	Bouna
10.	Boundiali	Boundiali
11.	Dabakala	Dabakala
12.	Daloa	Daloa
13.	Danané	Danané
14.	Dimbokro	Dimbokro
15.	Divo	Divo
16.	Ferkessedougou	Ferkessedougou
17.	Gagnoa	Gagnoa
18.	Guiglo	Guiglo
19.	Katiola	Katiola
20.	Korhogo	Korhogo
21.	Man	Man
22.	Odienné	Odienné
23.	Sassandra	Sassandra
24.	Séguéla	Séguéla
25.	Touba	Touba
26.	Bouaflé	Bouaflé

(1) JAMAICA

(2) The Government of Jamaica

(3) The Government of Jamaica

(4) Jamaica is an island in the Caribbean Sea, 100 miles west of Haiti and 90 miles south of Cuba.

(5) Kingston

(6) Jamaica comprises 13 administrative units; 1 independent city corporation (Kingston and St. Andrew/Kingston, capital) and 12 parishes.

Parishes		Capitals
1.	Hanover	Lucea
2.	St. James	Montego Bay
3.	Trelawny	Falmouth
4.	Westmoreland	Savanna-la-Mar
5.	St. Elizabeth	Black River
6.	St. Ann	St. Ann's Bay
7.	St. Mary	Port Maria
8.	Manchester	Mandeville
9.	Clarendon	May Pen
10.	St. Catherine	Spanish Town
11.	Portland	Port Antonio
12.	St. Thomas	Morant Bay

(1) JAN MAYEN

(2) Norwegian Territory of Jan Mayen

(3) Jan Mayen

(4) Jan Mayen is situated 300 miles NNE of Iceland.

(5) Jameson Bay

(6) Jan Mayen Island has no local units of government.

(1) JAPAN

(2) The Japanese Government

(3) Nippon Koku

(4) Japan is located in eastern Asia. Its islands are bounded by
the Sea of Japan on the west; by the Pacific Ocean on the
south and east; and by the U.S.S.R.'s Sakhalin Island toward
the north.

(5) Tokyo

(6) Japan comprises 47 administrative units known as prefectures
or "ken."

Ken	Capitals
1. Tokyo	Tokyo
2. Hokkaido	Sapporo
3. Aomori	Aomori
4. Iwate	Morioka
5. Miyagi	Sendai
6. Akita	Akita
7. Yamagata	Yamagata
8. Fukushima	Fukushima
9. Ibaraki	Mito
10. Tochigi	Utsunomiya
11. Gumma	Maebashi
12. Saitama	Urawa
13. Chiba	Chiba
14. Kanagawa	Yokohama
15. Niigata	Niigata
16. Toyama	Toyama
17. Ishikawa	Kanazawa
18. Fukui	Fukui

19.	Yamanashi	Kōfu
20.	Nagano	Nagano
21.	Gifu	Gifu
22.	Shizuoka	Shizuoka
23.	Aichi	Nagoya
24.	Mie	Tsu
25.	Shiga	Ōtsu
26.	Kyoto	Kyoto
27.	Osaka	Osaka
28.	Hyogo	Kōbe
29.	Nara	Nara
30.	Wakayama	Wakayama
31.	Tottori	Tottori
32.	Shimane	Matsue
33.	Okayama	Okayama
34.	Hiroshima	Hiroshima
35.	Yamaguchi	Yamaguchi
36.	Tokushima	Tokushima
37.	Kagawa	Takamatso
38.	Ehime	Matsuyama
39.	Kochi	Kochi
40.	Fukuoka	Fukuoka
41.	Saga	Saga
42.	Nagasaki	Nagasaki
43.	Kumamoto	Kumamoto
44.	Oita	Oita
45.	Miyazaki	Miyazaki
46.	Kagoshima	Kagoshima
47.	Okinawa	Naha

(1)   JOHNSTON ISLANDS

(2)   Johnston Atoll, a U.S. external possession

(3)   Johnston Atoll, a U.S. external possession

(4)   Johnston consists of two small islands about 1,150 kilometers southwest of Hawaii.

(5)   Johnston Atoll Settlement

(6)   Johnston Island is administered by the U.S. Defense Nuclear Agency. There are no local units of government.

(1) JORDAN

(2) The Hashemite Kingdom of Jordan

(3) Al Mamlaka al Urduniya al Hashemiyah

(4) Jordan lies between Israel and Iraq, with Syria to the north and Saudi Arabia to the south.

(5) Amman

(6) Jordan comprises 8 administrative units known as provinces or "muhafazat."

Muhafazat	Capitals
1. Irbid	Irbid
2. Al Asimah	Amman
3. Al Balqa	As Salt
4. Al Karak	Al Karak
5. Ma'an	Ma'an
6. Al Quds	Jerusalem
7. Al Khalil	Hebron
8. Nabulus	Nabulus

(1) JUAN FERNÁNDEZ

(2) Juan Fernández, a Dependency of Chile

(3) Juan Fernández

(4) Juan Fernández consists of three small islands of volcanic origin. It lies at a distance of 667 km. west of Valparaiso, Chile.

(5) Juan Bautista

(6) Juan Fernández has no local units of government.

(1) KAMPUCHEA (CAMBODIA)

(2) People's Republic of Kampuchea

(3) Sathearanakrath Pracheachon

(4) Kampuchea is bounded on the north by Laos and Thailand, on

the west by Thailand, on the east by Vietnam, and on the south by Kerala and the Gulf of Thailand.

(5) Phnom Penh

(6) Kampuchea comprises 27 administrative units; 21 provinces or "khet," 5 autonomous municipalities and 1 special capital region (Phnom Penh).

Khet	Capitals
1. Odongh Meanchey	Odongk
2. Vihear Suor	Khum Kampong Ampil
3. Ratanakiri	Lumphat
4. Stung Treng	Stung Treng
5. Preah Vihear	Phnum Tbeng Meanchey
6. Otdar Meanchey	Phumi Samraong
7. Batdambang	Batdambang
8. Pouthisat	Pouthisat
9. Kaoh Kong	Krong Kaoh Kong
10. Kampot	Kampot
11. Takev	Takev
12. Kandal	Takhmau
13. Prey Veng	Prey Veng
14. Svay Rieng	Svay Rieng
15. Kampong Speu	Kampong Speu
16. Kampong Chhnang	Kampong Chhnang
17. Kampong Thum	Kampong Thum
18. Kampong Cham	Kampong Cham
19. Kracheh	Kracheh
20. Mondol Kiri	Senmonoram
21. Siem Reap	Siem Reap

Autonomous Municipalities
22. Phnom Penh
23. Keb
24. Kirirom
25. Bok Kou
26. Kampong Saom

(1) KENYA

(2) Republic of Kenya

(3) Djumhuri ya Kenya

(4) Kenya is bounded by Ethiopia on the north, by Uganda on the west, by Tanzania on the south, and by Somalia and the Indian Ocean on the east.

(5) Nairobi

(6) Kenya comprises 8 administrative units; 1 national capital area (Nairobi) and 7 provinces.

Provinces	Capitals
1. Coast	Mombassa
2. Central	Nairobi
3. Eastern	Embu
4. Rift Valley	Nakuru
5. Western	Bungoma
6. Nyanza	Kisumu
7. North Eastern	Wajir

(1) KIRIBATI

(2) The Republic of Kiribati

(3) The Republic of Kiribati

(4) Kiribati is a group of 33 islands that lie astride the equator over an area of five million square miles of Pacific Ocean. The islands were formerly named the Gilbert Islands. They lie between 4° north and 3° south latitude and 172° to 177° east longitude.

(5) Bairiki, Tarawa Island

(6) Kiribati comprise 20 administrative units known as island councils.

Island Councils
1. Makin
2. Butaritari
3. Marakei
4. Abaiang
5. Tarawa
6. Maiana
7. Banaba
8. Abemama
9. Kuria
10. Aranuki
11. Nonouri
12. Tabiteuea
13. Beru
14. Nikunau
15. Onotoa
16. Tamana
17. Arorae
18. Washington

19. Fanning
20. Christmas

(1) KUWAIT

(2) State of Kuwait

(3) Dowlat al Kuwait

(4) Kuwait is situated on the northwestern coast of the Arabian Gulf.

(5) Kuwait City

(6) Kuwait comprises 4 administrative units known as governorates.

Governorates	Capitals
1. Ahmadi	Ahmadi
2. Hawalli	Hawalli
3. Kuwait	Kuwait
4. Jahra	Jahra

(1) LAOS

(2) The People's Democratic Republic of Laos

(3) Republique Democratique Populaire Lao

(4) Laos is bordered on the north by China, on the east by Vietnam, on the south by Kampuchea, and on the west by Thailand and Burma.

(5) Viangchan (Vientiane)

(6) Laos comprises 13 administrative units known as provinces.

Provinces	Capitals
1. Phong Saly	Phong Saly
2. Houa Khong	Nam Tha
3. Luang Prabang	Luang Prabang
4. Sayaboury	Sayaboury
5. Sam Neua	Sam Neua
6. Xieng Khouang	Xieng Khouang
7. Khammoung	Thakhek
8. Savannakhet	Savannakhet

9.	Saravane	Saravane
10.	Attopeu	Muong May
11.	Bassas	Pakse
12.	Borikane	Paksane
13.	Sithandone	Kong

(1) LEBANON

(2) Republic of Lebanon

(3) Al-Jumhouriya al-Lubnaniya

(4) Lebanon is bounded on the north and east by Syria, on the west by the Mediterranean, and on the south by Israel.

(5) Beirut

(6) Lebanon comprises 30 administrative units; 5 provinces or "muhafazat," and 25 districts.

Muhafazat		Capitals
1.	Beirut	Beirut
2.	Ash Shamal	Tripoli
3.	Jabal Lubnan	Beirut
4.	Al Biqa	Baalbek
5.	Al Janub	Tyre

Districts		Capitals
6.	Aley	Aley
7.	Amioun	Amioun
8.	Baabda	Baabda
9.	Baalbek	Baalbek
10.	Batoun	Batoun
11.	Bcharré	Bcharré
12.	Beït ed Dîne	Beït ed Dîne
13.	Beirut	Beirut
14.	Beni Jbail	Beni Jbail
15.	Halbâ	Halbâ
16.	Hasbaïya	Hasbaïya
17.	Hermel	Hermel
18.	Jbail	Jbail
19.	Jdaïdé	Jdaïdé
20.	Jounié	Jounié
21.	Jezzine	Jezzine
22.	Joub Jannine	Joub Jannine
23.	Marjoyoun	Marjoyoun
24.	Nabatiyé	Nabatiyé
25.	Rachaïya	Rachaïya

26.	Saïda	Saïda
27.	Sour	Sour
28.	Tripoli	Tripoli
29.	Zahlé	Zahlé
30.	Zgharta	Zgharta

(1) LESOTHO

(2) The Kingdom of Lesotho

(3) The Kingdom of Lesotho

(4) Lesotho is bounded on the west by South Africa's Orange Free State, on the north by Orange Free State and Natal, on the east by Natal and East Griqualand, and on the south by Cape Province.

(5) Maseru

(6) Lesotho comrpises 9 administrative units known as districts.

Districts	Capitals
1. Maseru	Maseru
2. Berea	Berea
3. Butha-Buthe	Butha-Buthe
4. Leribe	Leribe
5. Maketeng	Maketeng
6. Mohale's Hoek	Mohale's Hoek
7. Mokhotlong	Mokhotlong
8. Qacha's Nek	Qacha's Nek
9. Quthing	Quthing

(1) LIBERIA

(2) Republic of Liberia

(3) Republic of Liberia

(4) Liberia has about 350 miles of Atlantic Ocean coastline, extending from Sierra Leone, on the west, to the Ivory Coast, on the east.

(5) Monrovia

(6) Liberia comprises 10 administrative units; 1 federal capital district (Monrovia) and 9 counties.

87

Counties	Capitals
1. Bong	Gbanga
2. Grand Bassa	Buchanan
3. Grand Cape Mount	Robertsport
4. Grand Jide	Tchien
5. Lofa	Voinjama
6. Maryland	Harper
7. Montserrado	Monrovia
8. Nimba	Saniquellie
9. Sinoe	Greenville

(1) LIBYA

(2) People's Socialist Libyan Arab State of the Masses

(3) Al-Jamahiriyah Al-Arabiya Al-Libya Al-Shabiya Al-Ishtirakiya

(4) Libya is situated on the north coast of Africa between Egypt on the east and Tunisia on the west.

(5) Tripoli

(6) Libya comprises 13 administrative units; 3 provinces and 10 governorates.

Provinces	Capitals
1. Cyrenaica	Benghazi
2. Tripolitania	Tripoli
3. Fezzan	Sabhah

Governorates	Capitals
4. Tripoli	Tripoli
5. Benghazi	Benghazi
6. Zawia	Zawia
7. Misurata	Misurata
8. Homs	Homs
9. Gharian	Gharian
10. Jebel Akhdar	Jebel Akhdar
11. Derna	Derna
12. Sabhah	Sabhah
13. Kalig	Kalig

(1) LIECHTENSTEIN

(2) Principality of Liechtenstein

(3) Fürstentum Liechtenstein

(4) Liechtenstein is bounded on the east by Austria and on the
     west by Switzerland.

(5) Vaduz

(6) Liechtenstein comprises 11 administrative units known as com-
     munes or "gemeinden."

Gemeinden	Capitals
1. Vaduz	Vaduz
2. Balzers	Balzers
3. Planken	Planken
4. Schaan	Schaan
5. Triesen	Triesen
6. Triesenberg	Triesenberg
7. Eschen	Eschen
8. Gamprin	Gamprin
9. Mauren	Mauren
10. Ruggell	Ruggell
11. Schellenberg	Schellenberg

(1) LUXEMBOURG

(2) Grand Duchy of Luxembourg

(3) Grand-Duché de Luxembourg

(4) Luxembourg is bounded on the west by Belgium, on the south
     by France, and on the east by the Federal Republic of Ger-
     many.

(5) Luxembourg City

(6) Luxembourg comprises 15 administrative units; 3 districts and
     12 cantons.

Districts	Capitals
1. Luxembourg	Luxembourg
2. Diekirch	Diekirch
3. Gravenmacher	Gravenmacher

Cantons	Capitals
4. Capellen	Capellen
5. Esch-sur-Alzette	Esch-sur-Alzette
6. Luxembourg	Luxembourg
7. Mersch	Mersch

8.	Clervaux	Clervaux
9.	Diekirch	Diekirch
10.	Rédange	Rédange
11.	Vianden	Vianden
12.	Wiltz	Wiltz
13.	Gravenmacher	Gravenmacher
14.	Echternach	Echternach
15.	Remich	Remich

(1) MACAO

(2) Macao

(3) Macao

(4) Macao is located on a peninsula of the same name at the mouth of China's Canton River. It includes two small adjacent islands.

(5) Macao City

(6) Macao comprises 2 administrative units known as districts or "concelhos."

Concelhos	Capitals
1. Macao	Macao
2. Taipa and Coloane	Taipa

(1) MADAGASCAR

(2) The Democratic Republic of Madagascar

(3) Madagasikara

(4) Madagascar is situated off the southeast coast of Africa, from which it is separated by the Mozambique Channel.

(5) Antananarivo

(6) Madagascar comprises 6 administrative units known as provinces or "faritany."

Faritany	Capitals
1. Antananarivo	Antananarivo
2. Diégo-Suarez	Diégo-Suarez

3.	Fianarantsoa	Fianarantsoa
4.	Majunga	Majunga
5.	Toamasina	Toamasina
6.	Tulear	Tulear

(1) MALAWI

(2) Republic of Malawi

(3) Republic of Malawi

(4) Malawi lies along the southern and western shores of Lake Malawi and is bounded on the north by Tanzania, on the south by Mozambique, and on the west by Zambia.

(5) Lilongwe

(6) Malawi comprises 27 administrative units; 3 regions and 24 districts.

Regions		Capitals
1.	Northern	Mzuzu
2.	Central	Lilongwe
3.	Southern	Blantyre

Districts		Capitals
4.	Chitipa	Chitipa
5.	Karonga	Karonga
6.	Rumphi	Rumphi
7.	Mzimba	Mzimba
8.	Nkhata Bay	Nkata
9.	Nkhota Kota	Nkhota Kota
10.	Kasungu	Kasungu
11.	Ntchisi	Ntchisi
12.	Mchinji	Mchinji
13.	Dowa	Dowa
14.	Lilongwe	Lilongwe
15.	Salima	Salima
16.	Dedza	Dedza
17.	Mangoche	Mangoche
18.	Ncheu	Ncheu
19.	Kasupe	Kasupe
20.	Zomba	Zomba
21.	Mwanza	Mwanza
22.	Blantyre	Blantyre
23.	Chiradzulu	Chiradzulu
24.	Mulanje	Mulanje
25.	Chikwawa	Chikwawa

| 26. | Thyolo | Thyolo |
| 27. | Nsanje | Nsanje |

(1) MALAYSIA

(2) The Federation of Malaysia

(3) Persekutuan Tanah Melaya

(4) Malaysia occupies two distinct regions--the Malay Peninsula extending south-southeast from Thailand, and the northwestern coastal area of Borneo. It has land frontiers with Indonesia on the island of Borneo.

(5) Kuala Lumpur

(6) Malaysia comprises 14 administrative units; 1 federal capital territory (Kuala Lumpur) and 13 states.

States	Capitals
1. Johore	Johore Bahru
2. Kedah	Alor Star
3. Kelantan	Kota Bahru
4. Malacca	Malacca
5. Negri Sembilan	Seremban
6. Pahang	Kuantan
7. Penang and Province Wellesley	George Town
8. Perak	Ipoh
9. Perlis	Kangar
10. Sabah	Kota Kinabalu
11. Sarawak	Kuching
12. Selangor	Shah Alam
13. Trengganu	Kuala Tregganu

(1) MALDIVES

(2) The Republic of Maldives

(3) The Republic of Maldives

(4) Maldives lies about 420 miles southwest of Sri Lanka and comprises close to 1200 islands.

(5) Male

(6) Maldives comprises 19 administrative units known as districts or "atolls."

Atolls	Capitals
1. Ihavandiffulu	Ihavandiffulu
2. Malcolm	Malcolm
3. Powell	Powell
4. North Malosmadulu	North Malosmadulu
5. South Malosmadulu	South Malosmadulu
6. Horsburgh	Horsburgh
7. Ari	Ari
8. Nilandu	Nilandu
9. Kolumadulu	Kolumadulu
10. Tiladummati	Tiladummati
11. Miladummudulu	Miladummudulu
12. Fadiffolu	Fadiffolu
13. North Malé	North Malé
14. South Malé	South Malé
15. Felidu	Felidu
16. Mulaku	Mulaku
17. Haddummati	Haddummati
18. Suvadiva	Suvadiva
19. Addu	Addu

(1) MALI

(2) Republic of Mali

(3) République du Mali

(4) Mali is bounded on the northwest by Mauritania, on the northeast by Algeria, and on the east by Niger.

(5) Bamako

(6) Mali comprises 49 administrative units; 1 federal capital district (Bamako), 7 regions or "régions," and 41 counties or "cercles."

Regions	Capitals
1. Kayes	Kayes
2. Koulikoro	Koulikoro
3. Sikasso	Sikasso
4. Ségou	Ségou
5. Mopti	Mopti
6. Tombouctou	Tombouctou
7. Gao	Gao

Cercles	Capitals
8. Kayes	Kayes

93

9.	Bafoulabe	Bafoulabe
10.	Kenieba	Kenieba
11.	Kita	Kita
12.	Nioro	Nioro
13.	Yelimane	Yelimane
14.	Bamako	Bamako
15.	Banamba	Banamba
16.	Dioila	Dioila
17.	Kangaba	Kangaba
18.	Kolokani	Kolokani
19.	Koulikoro	Koulikoro
20.	Nara	Nara
21.	Ségou	Ségou
22.	San	San
23.	Macina	Macina
24.	Niona	Niona
25.	Tominian	Tominian
26.	Sikasso	Sikasso
27.	Bougouni	Bougouni
28.	Kadiolo	Kadiolo
29.	Kolondieba	Kolondieba
30.	Koutiala	Koutiala
31.	Yanfolila	Yanfolila
32.	Yorosso	Yorosso
33.	Mopto	Mopti
34.	Bankass	Bankass
35.	Djenne	Djenne
36.	Douentza	Douentza
37.	Koro	Koro
38.	Niafunke	Niafunke
39.	Tenenkou	Tenenkou
40.	Gao	Gao
41.	Ansongo	Ansongo
42.	Bourem	Bourem
43.	Dire	Dire
44.	Goundam	Goundam
45.	Kidal	Kidal
46.	Gourma-Rharous	Gourma-Rharous
47.	Timbuktu	Timbuktu
48.	Bandiagara	Bandiagara

(1) MALTA

(2) Republic of Malta

(3) Repubblika Ta Malta

(4) Malta is an island situated in the Mediterranean Sea about 93 km. south of Sicily.

94

(5)   Valletta

(6)   Malta comprises 6 administrative units known as statistical regions (nongovernmental divisions).

> Statistical Regions
> 1.   Inner Harbour
> 2.   Northern
> 3.   Outer Harbour
> 4.   Southeastern
> 5.   Western
> 6.   Gozo and Comino

(1)   MARSHALL ISLANDS

(2)   The State of The Marshall Islands

(3)   The State of The Marshall Islands

(4)   The Marshalls are a double chain of 34 coral atolls lying between 5° and 15° north latitude and 162° and 172° east longitude.

(5)   Majuro

(6)   Marshall Islands comprise 25 administrative units known as municipalities.

> Municipalities
> 1.   Ailinglapalap
> 2.   Ailuk
> 3.   Arno
> 4.   Aur
> 5.   Ebon
> 6.   Jaluit
> 7.   Kili
> 8.   Kwajalein
> 9.   Ebeye (Village)
> 10.   Lae
> 11.   Lib
> 12.   Likiep
> 13.   Darrit Uliga Dalap
> 14.   Laura
> 15.   Maloelap
> 16.   Mejit
> 17.   Mili
> 18.   Namorik
> 19.   Namu

20. Rongelap
21. Ujae
22. Ujelang
23. Utirik
24. Wotho
25. Wotje

(1) MARTINIQUE

(2) French Overseas Department of Martinique

(3) Martinique Département Outremer

(4) Martinique is situated in the Lesser Antilles between Dominica
     and St. Lucia. It occupies an area of 425 square miles, being
     50 miles long and 22 miles wide.

(5) Fort-de-France

(6) Martinique comprises 37 administrative units; 3 arrondissements
     and 34 communes.

Arrondissements	Capitals
1. Fort-de-France	Fort-de-France
2. Sainte-Marie	Sainte-Marie
3. Lamentin	Lamentin

Communes
4. Fort-de-France
5. Sainte-Marie
6. Lamentin
7. Robert
8. François
9. Rivière Pilote
10. Gros Morne
11. Lorrain
12. Saint-Joseph
13. Trinite
14. Vauclin
15. Saint-Esprit
16. Schoelcher
17. Rivière Salée
18. Saint-Pierre
19. Marin
20. Ducos
21. Basse Pointe
22. Morne Rouge
23. Sainte-Luce

24. Carbet
25. Marigot
26. Trois Îlets
27. Anses d'Arlets
28. Sainte-Anne
29. Precheur
30. Diamant
31. Macouba
32. Morne Vert
33. Ajoupa Bouillon
34. Fonds Saint-Denis
35. Case-Pilote
36. Bellefontaine
37. Grand-Rivière

(1) MAURITANIA

(2) The Islamic Republic of Mauritania

(3) République Islamique de Mauritanie

(4) Mauritania is located in Western Africa. It is bounded by the Atlantic Ocean and southern Morocco on the west; by Algeria on the north and northeast; by Mali on the east; and by Senegal on the south.

(5) Nouakchott

(6) Mauritania comprises 13 administrative units; 1 federal capital district (Nouakchott) and 12 regions "wilayas."

Wilayas	Capitals
1. Hodh el Charqui	Néma
2. Hodh el Gharbi	Aïoun el Atrous
3. Assaba	Kiffa
4. Gorgol	Kaédi
5. Brakna	Aleg
6. Trarza	Rosso
7. Adrar	Atar
8. Dakhlet-Nouadhibou	Nouadhibou
9. Tagant	Tidjikja
10. Guidimaka	Sélibaby
11. Tiris Zemmour	F'Derik
12. Inchiri	Akjoujt

(1) MAURITIUS

(2) Mauritius

(3) Mauritius

(4) Mauritius is situated 20° south latitude and 57½° east longitude in the Indian Ocean approximately 1,240 miles from Durban.

(5) Port Louis

(6) Mauritius comprises 11 administrative units known as districts.

Districts	Capitals
1. Black River	Grand Rivière Noire
2. Flacq	Centre de Flacq
3. Grand-Port	Rose Belle
4. Moka	Moka
5. Pamplemousses	Mapou
6. Plaines Wilhelms	Curepipe
7. Port-Louis	Port-Louis
8. Rivière-du-Rempart	Goodlands
9. Savanne	Chemin Grenier
10. Îles Agalega-St. Brandon	St. Brandon
11. Île Rodriques	Île Rodriques

(1) MAYOTTE

(2) Territorial Collectivity of Mayotte

(3) Mayotte Collectivité Territoriale

(4) One of the Comoro Islands but separate from them in administration, Mayotte is situated in the Mozambique Channel midway between Madagascar and Mozambique.

(5) Mtsamboro

(6) Mayotte comprises 17 administrative units known as cantons.

Cantons
1. Acoua
2. Bandraboua
3. Bandrele
4. Boueni
5. Chiconi
6. Chirongoi

7. Dembeni
8. Dzaoudzi
9. Kani-Keli
10. Koungou
11. Mamoudzou
12. Mtsamboro
13. M'Tsangamouji
14. Ouangani
15. Pamandzi
16. Sada
17. Tsingoni

(1) MEXICO

(2) The Federal Republic of Mexico

(3) Estados Unidos Mexicanos

(4) Mexico is at the southern extremity of North America and is bounded on the north by the U.S.A., on the west and southwest by the Pacific, on the south by Guatemala and Belize, and on the east by the Gulf of Mexico.

(5) Mexico City

(6) Mexico comprises 32 administrative units; 1 federal capital district (Distrito Federal/Mexico City, capital) and 31 states.

States	Capitals
1. Aguascalientes	Aguascalientes
2. Baja California Norte	Mexicali
3. Baja California Sur	La Paz
4. Campeche	Campeche
5. Chiapas	Tuxtla Gutiérrez
6. Chihuahua	Chihuahua
7. Coahuila	Saltillo
8. Colima	Colima
9. Durango	Victoria de Durango
10. Guanajuato	Guanajuato
11. Guerrero	Chilpanchingo de los Bravos
12. Hidalgo	Pachuca de Soto
13. Jalisco	Guadalajara
14. México	Toluca de Lerdo
15. Michoachán	Morelia
16. Morelos	Cuernavaca
17. Nayarit	Tepic
18. Nuevo León	Monterrey
19. Oaxaca	Oaxaca de Juárez

20.	Puebla	Heróica Puebla de Zaragoza
21.	Querétaro	Querétaro
22.	Quintana Roo	Chetumal
23.	San Luis Potosí	San Luis Potosí
24.	Sinaloa	Culiacán
25.	Sonora	Hermosillo
26.	Tabasco	Villa Hermosa
27.	Tamaulipas	Ciudad Victoria
28.	Tlaxcala	Tlaxcala de Xicohténcatl
29.	Veracruz	Jalapa Enríquez
30.	Yucantán	Mérida
31.	Zacatecas	Zacatecas

(1)   MICRONESIA, FEDERATED STATES OF

(2)   The Federated States of Micronesia

(3)   The Federated States of Micronesia

(4)   The Federated States of Micronesia are in the Western Pacific and comprise four of the six units of the Trust Territory of the Pacific.

(5)   Kolonia, Ponape Island

(6)   Micronesia comprises 4 administrative units known as states.

States	Capitals
1. Kosrae	Lelu
2. Yap	Yap Town
3. Ponape	Kolonia
4. Truk	Moen

(1)   MIDWAY ISLANDS

(2)   Midway Islands, U.S. External Territory

(3)   Midway Islands, U.S. External Territory

(4)   The Midway Islands consist of two small islands at the western end of the Hawaiian Islands chain.

(5)   Midway Islands

(6)   The Midway Islands are administered by the U.S. Navy and contain no local government units.

(1) MONACO

(2) Principality of Monaco

(3) Principauté de Monaco

(4) Monaco is a small principality situated on the shores of the Mediterranean and extending inland to the slopes of the Alpes-Maritimes.

(5) Monaco-Ville

(6) Monaco comprises 4 administrative units known as communal quarters.

Communal Quarters	Capitals
1. Monte Carlo	Monte Carlo
2. La Condamine	La Condamine
3. Monaco-Ville	Monaco-Ville
4. Fontvieille	Fontvieille

(1) MONGOLIA

(2) Mongolian People's Republic

(3) Bügd Nayramdakh Mongol Ard Uls

(4) Mongolia is bounded on the north by the U.S.S.R., and on the east, south, and west by China.

(5) Ulan Bator

(6) Mongolia comprises 21 administrative units; 3 special municipalities and 18 provinces or "aimag."

Special Municipalities
1. Ulan Bator
2. Darhan
3. Erdenet

Aimag	Capitals
4. Arhangay	Tsetserleg
5. Bayanhongor	Bayanhongor
6. Bayan-Ölgiy	Ölgiy
7. Bulgan	Bulgan
8. Dornod	Choybalsan
9. Dornogov́	Saynshand
10. Dundgov́	Mandalgov́

11.	Dzavhan	Uliastay
12.	Gov́-altay	Altay
13.	Hentiy	Öndörhaan
14.	Hovd	Hovd
15.	Hövsgöl	Mörön
16.	Ömnögov́	Dalandzadgad
17.	Övörhangay	Arvayheer
18.	Selenge	Sühbaatar
19.	Sühbaatar	Baruun Urt
20.	Töv	Dzuun Mod
21.	Uvs	Ulaangom

(1) MONTSERRAT

(2) Crown Colony of Montserrat

(3) Crown Colony of Montserrat

(4) Montserrat is situated in the Caribbean Sea 25 miles southwest of Antigua.

(5) Plymouth

(6) Montserrat comprises 10 administrative units; 3 parishes and 7 districts.

Parishes		Capitals
1.	St. Peter	Salem
2.	St. George	Harris
3.	St. Anthony	Plymouth

Districts
4. Plymouth
5. Southern
6. Northwestern
7. Central
8. Windward
9. Eastern
10. Northern

(1) MOROCCO

(2) Kingdom of Morocco

(3) Al-Mamlaka al-Maghrebia

(4) Morocco is the westernmost of the three North African countries and has an extensive coastline facing both the Atlantic and the Mediterranean.

(5) Rabat

(6) Morocco comprises 43 administrative units; 6 municipal prefectures and 37 provinces.

Municipal Prefectures
1. Casablanca-Anfa
2. Hay-Mohamed-Aïn Sebaa
3. Aïn-Chock-Hay-Hassani
4. Ben-Msik-Sidi-Othmane
5. Mohamedia
6. Rabat-Salé

Provinces	Capitals
7. Agadir	Agadir
8. Al-Hoceima	Al-Hoceima
9. Azilal	Azilal
10. Béni Mellal	Béni Mellal
11. Boujdour	Boujdour
12. Boulemane	Boulemane
13. Chaouen	Chaouen
14. El Jadida	El Jadida
15. El Kellâa Sraghna	El Kellâa Sraghna
16. Essaouira	Essaouira
17. Es Semara	Es Semara
18. Fès	Fès
19. Figuig	Figuig
20. Khémisset	Khémisset
21. Kénitra	Kénitra
22. Khénifra	Khénifra
23. Khouribga	Khouribga
24. Laâyoune	Laâyoune
25. Marrakech	Marrakech
26. Meknès	Meknès
27. Nador	Nador
28. Ouarzazate	Ouarzazate
29. Oujda	Oujda
30. Safi	Safi
31. Settat	Settat
32. Tanger	Tanger
33. Tan-Tan	Tan-Tan
34. Taza	Taza
35. Tétouan	Tétouan
36. Tiznit	Tiznit
37. Ben Slimane	Ben Slimane
38. Errachidia	Errachidia

39. Guelmim	Guelmim
40. Oued Ed-Dahab	Oued Ed-Dahab
41. Ta-Ta	Ta-Ta
42. Taounate	Taounate
43. Ifrane	Ifrane

(1) MOZAMBIQUE

(2) The People's Republic of Mozambique

(3) República de Moçambique

(4) Mozambique is bounded on the east by the Indian Ocean, on the south by South Africa, on the southwest by Swaziland, on the west by South Africa and Zimbabwe, and on the north by Zambia, Malawi, and Tanzania.

(5) Maputo

(6) Mozambique comprises 10 administrative units known as provinces.

Provinces	Capitals
1. Maputo	Maputo
2. Gaza	Vila de João Belo
3. Inhambane	Inhambane
4. Manica	Beira
5. Sofala	Beira
6. Tete	Tete
7. Zambézia	Quelimane
8. Moçambique	Nampula
9. Cabo Delgado	Porto Amélia
10. Niassa	Vila Cabral

(1) NAMIBIA

(2) Namibia

(3) Namibia

(4) Namibia stretches from the southern border of Angola to part of the northern and northwestern borders of South Africa's Cape Province; and from the Atlantic Ocean in the west to Botswana in the east.

(5) Windhoek

(6) Namibia comprises 37 administrative units; 11 administrative
     districts and 26 magisterial districts.

Administrative Districts	Capitals
1. Kaokoland	Sarusas
2. Ovamboland	Oshakati
3. Kavango	Rundu
4. Caprivi West	Omega
5. Caprivi East	Katima Mulilo
6. Bushmanland	Baraka
7. Hereroland West	Okakarara
8. Hereroland East	Gam
9. Damaraland	Fransfontein
10. Rehoboth	Rehoboth
11. Namaland	Namaland

Magisterial Districts	Capitals
12. Koakoland	Opuwo
13. Swakopmund	Swakopmund
14. Walvis Bay	Walvis Bay
15. Lüderitz	Lüderitz
16. Bethanien	Bethanien
17. Karasburg	Karasburg
18. Keetmanshoop	Keetmanshoop
19. Mariental	Mariental
20. Maltanhöhe	Maltanhöhe
21. Rehoboth	Rehoboth
22. Windhoek	Windhoek
23. Karibib	Karibib
24. Gobabio	Gobabio
25. Okahandja	Okahandja
26. Omaruru	Omaruru
27. Otjiwarongo	Otjiwarongo
28. Damaraland	Fransfontein
29. Hereroland Wes	Okakarara
30. Hereroland Oos	Gam
31. Grootfontein	Otavi
32. Outjo	Outjo
33. Tsumeb	Tsumeb
34. Boesmanland	Baraka
35. Kavango	Dossa
36. Caprivi	Katima Mulilo
37. Owambo	Ondangwa

(1) NAURU

(2) Republic of Nauru

(3) Naoero

105

(4) Nauru Island is an oval-shaped coral island in the Pacific Ocean situated at 0°32' south latitude and 166°55' east longitude. It is northeast of the Solomons, 26 miles south of the equator.

(5) Yaren

(6) Nauru comprises 14 administrative districts.

Districts	Capitals
1. Ewa	Anna
2. Anetan	Ronawi
3. Ijuw	Ijuw
4. Anibar	Anibar
5. Meneng	Meneng
6. Yaren	Makwa
7. Boe	Boe
8. Aiwo	Yangor
9. Denigomodu	Denigomodu
10. Nibok	Nibok
11. Uaboe	Domaneab
12. Baiti	Baiti
13. Buada	Buada
14. Anibare	Anibare

(1) NEPAL

(2) Kingdom of Nepál

(3) Nepál Alhirajya

(4) Nepál is bounded on the north by Tibet, on the east by India's Sikkim and West Bengal, and on the south and west by India's Bihar and Uttar Pradesh.

(5) Kathmandu

(6) Nepal comprises 14 administrative units known as zones or "anchal."

Anchal	Capitals
1. Mechi	Ilam
2. Kosi	Biratnager
3. Sagarmatha	Rajbiraj
4. Janakpur	Jaleswar
5. Bagmati	Kathmandu
6. Narayani	Bhimphedi
7. Gandaki	Pokhara

106

8.	Lumbini	Bhairawa
9.	Dhaulagiri	Baglung
10.	Rapati	Sallyan
11.	Karnali	Jumla
12.	Bheri	Nepalganj
13.	Seti	Dhangarhi
14.	Mahakali	Dandeldhura

(1) NETHERLANDS

(2) The Kingdom of The Netherlands

(3) Koninkrijk der Nederlanden

(4) The Netherlands is bounded on the north and west by the North Sea, on the south by Belgium, and on the east by the Federal Republic of Germany.

(5) Amsterdam

(6) Netherlands comprises 11 administrative units known as provinces.

Provinces		Capitals
1.	Groningen	Groningen
2.	Friesland	Leeuwarden
3.	Drenthe	Assen
4.	Overijssel	Zwolle
5.	Gelderland	Arnhem
6.	Utrecht	Utrecht
7.	Noord-Holland	Amsterdam
8.	Zuid-Holland	s'Gravenhage
9.	Zeeland	Middleburg
10.	Noord-Brabant	s'Hertogenbosch
11.	Limburg	Maastricht

(1) NETHERLANDS ANTILLES

(2) The Netherlands Antilles

(3) De Nederlandse Antillen

(4) The Netherlands Antilles comprises two groups of islands: the Leewards, north of the Venezuelan coast and the Windwards, east of Puerto Rico.

(5) Willemstad

(6) The Netherlands Antilles comprises 4 administrative units known as island councils.

Island Councils	Capitals
1. Curaçao	Willemstad
2. Aruba	Oranjestad
3. Bonaire	Kralendijk
4. Windward Islands	Philipsburg (St. Maarten)

(1) NEW CALEDONIA

(2) French Overseas Territory of New Caledonia

(3) La Nouvelle Calédonie Territoire d'Outremer

(4) This group of islands is located between 19° and 23° south latitude and 163° and 168° east longitude in the Pacific.

(5) Nouméa

(6) New Caledonia comprises 35 administrative units; 31 districts or "circonscriptions" and 4 subdivisions.

Circonscriptions	Capitals
1. Boulouparis	Boulouparis
2. Bourail	Bourail
3. Canala	Canala
4. Dumbea	Dumbea
5. Farino	Farino
6. Hienghène	Hienghène
7. Houailou	Houailou
8. Ouégoa	Ouégoa
9. Ouvéa	Fayoué
10. Paita	Paita
11. Poindimié	Poindimié
12. Ponérihouen	Ponérihouen
13. Pouembout	Pouembout
14. Pouebo	Pouebo
15. Poya	Poya
16. Sarraméa	Sarraméa
17. Thio	Thio
18. Toubo	Toubo
19. Îles Belep	Wala
20. Îles des Pins	Vao
21. Kaala-Gomen	Kaala-Gomen
22. Kone	Kone

23.	Koumac	Koumac
24.	La Foa	La Foa
25.	Lifou et Maré	Tadine
26.	Maré	Maré
27.	Moindou	Moindou
28.	Mont-Dare	Mont-Dare
29.	Nouméa	Nouméa
30.	Voh	Voh
31.	Yate	Yate

Subdivisions		Capitals
32.	Sud	La Foa, Nouméa I.
33.	Ouest	Koné
34.	Est	Poindimié
35.	Îles Loyauté	Wé, Lifou I.

(1) NEW ZEALAND

(2) The Dominion of New Zealand

(3) The Dominion of New Zealand

(4) New Zealand lies southeast of Australia in the South Pacific.

(5) Wellington

(6) New Zealand comprises 240 administrative units; 99 county
councils, 132 borough councils, 5 town councils, and 4
district councils.

Counties
1.   Mangonui
2.   Whangaroa
3.   Hokianga
4.   Bay of Islands
5.   Whangarei
6.   Hobson
7.   Otamatea
8.   Rodney
9.   Waiheke
10.   Great Barrier Islands
11.   Franklin
12.   Raglan
13.   Waikato
14.   Waipa
15.   Otorohanga
16.   Taumarunui
17.   Hauraki Plains

18. Ohinemuri
19. Piako
20. Matamata
21. Tauranga
22. Rotorua
23. Taupo
24. Opotiki
25. Waiapu
26. Waikohu
27. Cook
28. Wairoa
29. Hawke's Bay
30. Waipawa
31. Dannevirke
32. Woodville
33. Clifton
34. Taranaki
35. Inglewood
36. Stratford
37. Egmont
38. Eltham
39. Waimate West
40. Hawera
41. Patea
42. Waimarino
43. Waitotara
44. Wanganui
45. Rangitikei
46. Kiwitea
47. Pohangina
48. Oroua
49. Manawatu
50. Kairanga
51. Horowhenua
52. Hutt
53. Pahiatua
54. Eketahuna
55. Masterton
56. Wairarapa South
57. Featherston
58. Marlborough
59. Kaikouri
60. Golden Bay
61. Waimea
62. Buller
63. Inangahua
64. Grey
65. Westland
66. Amuri
67. Cheviot
68. Waipara

69. Ashley
70. Rangiora
71. Eyre
72. Oxford
73. Malvern
74. Papurua
75. Waimairi
76. Heathcote
77. Mt. Herbert
78. Akaroa
79. Chatham Islands
80. Wairewa
81. Ellesmere
82. Ashburton
83. Strathallon
84. Mackenzie
85. Waimate
86. Waitaki
87. Waihemo
88. Waikouaiti
89. Taieri
90. Bruce
91. Clutha
92. Tuapeka
93. Maniototo
94. Vincent
95. Lake
96. Southland
97. Wallace
98. Fiord
99. Steward Island

Boroughs
100. Kaitaia
101. Kaikohe
102. Whagarei (city)
103. Dargaville
104. Helensville
105. East Coast Bays (city)
106. Takapuna (city)
107. Devonport
108. Northcote
109. Birkenhead
110. Waitemata (city)
111. Henderson
112. Glen Eden
113. New Lynn
114. Auckland (city)
115. Newmarket
116. Mt. Albert
117. Mt. Eden

118. Mt. Roskill
119. Onehunga
120. One Tree Hill
121. Ellerslie
122. Mt. Wellington
123. Howick
124. Otahuhu
125. Papatoetoe (city)
126. Manukau (city)
127. Papakura (city)
128. Pukekohe
129. Waiuku
130. Tuakau
131. Huntley
132. Cambridge
133. Ngaruawahia
134. Hamilton (city)
135. Te Awamutu
136. Taumarunui
137. Paeroa
138. Waihi
139. Te Aroha
140. Morrinsville
141. Matamata
142. Putaruru
143. Tokoroa
144. Mt. Maunganui
145. Tauranga (city)
146. Te Puke
147. Rotorua (city)
148. Taupo
149. Kawerau
150. Murupara
151. Gisborne (city)
152. Wairoa
153. Napier (city)
154. Hastings (city)
155. Havelock North
156. Waipawa
157. Dannevirke
158. Woodville
159. Waitara
160. New Plymouth (city)
161. Inglewood
162. Stratford
163. Eltham
164. Hawera
165. Patea
166. Ohakune
167. Raetihi
168. Wanganui (city)

169. Taihape
170. Marton
171. Feilding
172. Foxton
173. Palmerston North (city)
174. Levin
175. Otaki
176. Kapiti
177. Upper Hutt (city)
178. Lower Hutt (city)
179. Petone
180. Eastbourne
181. Porirua (city)
182. Tawa
183. Wellington (city)
184. Pahiatua
185. Masterton
186. Carterton
187. Greytown
188. Featherston
189. Martinborough
190. Picton
191. Blenheim
192. Nelson (city)
193. Richmond
194. Motueka
195. Westport
196. Runanga
197. Greymouth
198. Hokitika
199. Rangiora
200. Kaiapoi
201. Riccarton
202. Christchurch (city)
203. Lyttelton
204. Ashburton
205. Geraldine
206. Temuka
207. Timaru (city)
208. Waimate
209. Oamaru
210. Port Chalmers
211. Dunedin (city)
212. St. Kilda
213. Green Island
214. Mosgiel
215. Milton
216. Kaitangata
217. Balclutha
218. Tapanui
219. Lawrence

220. Roxburgh
221. Naseby
222. Alexandra
223. Cromwell
224. Arrowtown
225. Queenstown
226. Gore
227. Mataura
228. Winton
229. Invercargill (city)
230. Bluff
231. Riverton

Town Councils
232. Hikurangi
233. Manaia
234. Waverley
235. Wyndham
236. Otautau

District Councils
237. Thames Coromandel
238. Waipukurau
239. Waitomo
240. Whakatane

(1) NICARAGUA

(2) Republic of Nicaragua

(3) República de Nicaragua

(4) Nicaragua is the largest in area of the Central American re-
    publics. Its coastline runs 336 miles on the Atlantic and 219
    miles on the Pacific.

(5) Managua

(6) Nicaragua comprises 17 administrative units; 1 special district
    or "comarca" (Cabo Gracias a Dios/Zelaya, capital) and 16
    departments.

Departments	Capitals
1. Boaco	Boaco
2. Corazo	Jinotepe
3. Chinandega	Chinandega
4. Chontales	Juigalpa
5. Estei	Estei

6.	Grenada	Grenada
7.	Jinotega	Jinotega
8.	Leon	Leon
9.	Madriz	Somoto
10.	Managua	Managua
11.	Masaya	Masaya
12.	Matagulpa	Matagulpa
13.	Nueva Segovia	Octotal
14.	Rio San Juan	San Carlos
15.	Rivas	Rivas
16.	Zelaya	Bluefields

(1) NIGER

(2) Republic of Niger

(3) République du Niger

(4) Niger is bounded on the north by Algeria and Libya, on the east by Chad, on the south by Nigeria, on the southwest by Dahomey and Upper Volta, and on the west by Mali.

(5) Niamey

(6) Niger comprises 38 administrative units; 7 departments and 31 arrondissements.

Departments	Capitals
1. Niamey	Niamey
2. Dosso	Dosso
3. Tahoua	Tahoua
4. Maradi	Maradi
5. Zinder	Zinder
6. Agadez	Agadez
7. Diffa	Nguigmi

Arrondissements	Capitals
8. Birni N'Konni	Birni N'Konni
9. Dogondoutchi	Dogondoutchi
10. Filingue	Filingue
11. Madsoua	Madsoua
12. Magaria	Magaria
13. Tessaoua	Tessaoua
14. Tillaberi	Tillaberi
15. Goure	Goure
16. Tera	Tera
17. Iférouane	Iférouane
18. Bilma	Bilma

115

19.	N'Gourti	N'Guigmi
20.	Maine Soroa	Maine
21.	Goure	Goure
22.	Tanout	Tanout
23.	Zinder	Zinder
24.	Matameye	Matameye
25.	Magaria	Magaria
26.	Mayahi	Mayahi
27.	Dakoro	Dakoro
28.	Tchin Taberarden	Tchin Tabaraden
29.	Keita	Keita
30.	Tahoua	Tahoua
31.	Ilhela	Ilhela
32.	Loga	Loga
33.	Birni N'Gaoure	Dosso
34.	Gaya	Gaya
35.	Niamey	Niamey
36.	Tera	Tera
37.	Ouallam	Ouallam
38.	Say	Say

(1) NIGERIA

(2) The Federal Republic of Nigeria

(3) The Federal Republic of Nigeria

(4) Nigeria is bounded on the west by Benin, on the north by Niger, on the east by Cameroon, and on the south by the Atlantic Ocean.

(5) Lagos

(6) Nigeria comprises 19 administrative units known as states.

States		Capitals
1.	Ogun	Abeokuta
2.	Ondo	Akure
3.	Oyo	Ibaden
4.	Bendel	Benin City
5.	Lagos	Ikeja
6.	Anambra	Enugu
7.	Imo	Owerri
8.	Cross River	Calabar
9.	Rivers	Port Harcourt
10.	Kwara	Ilorin
11.	Benue	Makurdi
12.	Plateau	Jos

13.	Niger	Minna
14.	Sokoto	Sokoto
15.	Gongola	Jimeta
16.	Borno	Maiduguri
17.	Kaduna	Kaduna
18.	Bauchi	Bauchi
19.	Kano	Kano

(1) NIUE

(2) Niue, a New Zealand self-governing territory

(3) Niue, a New Zealand self-governing territory

(4) Niue is located 19° south latitude and 169° west longitude, about 480 kilometers east of Tonga, and about 560 kilometers southeast of Samoa.

(5) Alofi

(6) Niue Island comprises 14 administrative units known as village councils.

Village Councils
1. Matulau
2. Toi
3. Lakepa
4. Liku
5. Hakupu
6. Vaiea
7. Avatela
8. Tamakautonga
9. Fonuakula
10. Alofi
11. Makefu
12. Tuapa
13. Namukulu
14. Hikutavake

(1) NORFOLK ISLAND

(2) Norfolk Island, an Australian External Territory

(3) Norfolk Island, an Australian External Territory

(4) Norfolk is located 29°2' south latitude and 167°57' east longitude. It is 1676 km. east-north-east of Sydney and 1065 km. north of Auckland.

(5) Kingston

(6) Norfolk Island comprises 14 administrative divisions; 4 settlements and 10 reserves.

<u>Settlements</u>
1. Cascade
2. Burt Pine
3. Middlegate
4. Kingston

<u>Reserves</u>
5. Point Hunter
6. Kingston Common
7. Bumbora
8. Rocky Point
9. Headstone
10. Selwyn
11. Mt. Pitt
12. Cascade
13. Point Blackbourne
14. Ball Bay

(1) NORTH KOREA

(2) Democratic People's Republic of Korea

(3) Chosun Minchu-chui Immin Konghwa-guk

(4) North Korea is located in Northeastern Asia. It is bounded by China on the north; by the Sea of Japan on the east; by South Korea on the south; and by the Yellow Sea on the west.

(5) Pyongyang

(6) North Korea comprises 13 administrative units; 4 special municipalities and 9 provinces.

<u>Special Municipalities</u>
1. Pyongyang
2. Chongjin
3. Hamheung
4. Kaesong

Provinces	Capitals
5. Pyongan-Namdo	Nampo
6. Pyongan-Pukto	Sinuiji
7. Jagang-do	Kanggye
8. Hwanghai-namdo	Haeju
9. Hwanghai-pukto	Sariwon
10. Kangwon-do	Wonsan
11. Hamgyong-namdo	Hamheung
12. Hamgyong-pukto	Chongjin
13. Yanggang-do	Hyesan

(1) NORTH YEMEN

(2) The Yemen Arab Republic

(3) Al Jamhuriya al Arabiya al Yamaniya

(4) Yemen is located in southwestern Asia on the Arabian Peninsula. It is bounded by Saudi Arabia on the north; by Saudi Arabia and South Yemen on the east and south; and by the Red Sea on the West.

(5) San'a

(6) North Yemen comprises 10 administrative units known as governorates or "alwiyah."

Alwiyah	Capitals
1. San'a	San'a
2. Hodeida	Hodeida
3. Taiz	Taiz
4. Saidah	Saidah
5. Hajjah	Hajjah
6. Dhamar	Dhamar
7. Ibb	Ibb
8. Al Baidha	Al Baidha
9. Al Mahwit	Al Mahwit
10. Marib	Marib

(1) NORTHERN MARIANA ISLANDS

(2) Commonwealth of The Northern Marianas

(3) Commonwealth of The Northern Marianas

(4) The Northern Marianas are a chain of 16 islands extending for some 480 kilometers from north to south. The main island, Saipan, is towards the south of the group at 15°12' north latitude and 145°43' east longitude.

(5) Susupe, Saipan Island

(6) Northern Marianas comprise 16 administrative units; 4 island constituencies and 12 subdivisions.

Island Constituencies	Capitals
1. Saipan	Susupe
2. Rota	Rota
3. Tinian	Tinian
4. Northern Islands	Pagan Island

Subdivisions
  5. Agrihan Island
  6. Pagan Island
  7. Rota Municipality
  8. Chalon Kanao Town
  9. Gualo-Roi-Garapan Village
 10. Olei Village
 11. San Antonio Village
 12. San Rogue Village
 13. San Vincente Village
 14. Susupe Village
 15. Tanapac Village
 16. Tinian Municipality

(1) NORWAY

(2) The Kingdom of Norway

(3) Kongeriket Norge

(4) Norway is bounded on the north by the Arctic Ocean; on the east by the U.S.S.R., Finland, and Sweden; on the south by the Skagerrak Straits, and on the west by the North Sea.

(5) Oslo

(6) Norway comprises 20 administrative units; 1 special capital municipality (Oslo) and 19 counties.

Counties	Capitals
1. Østfold	Moss
2. Akerhus	Baerhum

3.	Hedmark	Hamar
4.	Oppland	Lillehammer
5.	Buskerud	Drammen
6.	Vestfold	Tønsberg
7.	Telemark	Skien
8.	Aust-Agder	Arondal
9.	Vest-Agder	Kristiansand
10.	Rogaland	Stavanger
11.	Hordaland	Voss
12.	Sogn og Fjordane	Hermansverk
13.	Møre og Romsdal	Moldo
14.	Sør-Trøndelag	Trondheim
15.	Nord-Trøndelag	Steinkjor
16.	Nordland	Bodø
17.	Troms	Tromsø
18.	Finnmark	Vadsø
19.	Oslo	Oslo

(1)   OMAN

(2)   The Sultanate of Oman

(3)   Saltanat ^cUman

(4)   Oman is situated in southeast Arabia. Its coastline extends
from the Trucial Emirate of Ras al Khaimah on the western
side of the Musandum Peninsula to the People's Republic of
Yemen to the south.

(5)   Muscat

(6)   Oman comprises 39 administrative units; 1 federal capital municipality (Muscat), 1 federal province (Dhofar/Salalah, capital), and 37 governorates or "wilayats."

Wilayats		Capitals
1.	Dank	Dank
2.	Ibri	Ibri
3.	Nakhl and Wadi Maawal	Nakhl
4.	Rustaq	Rustaq
5.	Awabi	Awabi
6.	Bahla	Bahla
7.	Nizwa	Nizwa
8.	Birkat al Mawz	Birkat al Mawz
9.	Manah	Manah
10.	Adam	Adam
11.	Al Mudaibi	Al Mudaibi
12.	Ibra	Ibra

13.	Wadi Bani Khalid	Wadi Bani Khalid
14.	Al Mudhayrib	Al Mudhayrib
15.	Biddiya	Biddiya
16.	Bilad Bani Bu Hassan	Bilad Bani Bu Hassan
17.	Kamil and Wafi	Kamil
18.	Wadi Dimma	Wadi Dimma
19.	Jalan and Bilad Bani Bu Ali	Bilad Bani Bu Ali
20.	Sur	Sur
21.	Quriyat	Quriyat
22.	Bid Bid	Bid Bid
23.	Sumail	Sumail
24.	Izki	Izki
25.	Buraymi	Buraymi
26.	Mahadhah	Mahadhah
27.	Barka	Barka
28.	Al Masanaa	Al Masanna
29.	Suwaiq	Suwaiq
30.	Al Khabura	Al Khabura
31.	Saham	Saham
32.	Sohar	Sohar
33.	Liwa	Liwa
34.	Shinas	Shinas
35.	Khasab	Khasab
36.	Dibbah	Dibbah
37.	Bukh	Bukh

(1) PAKISTAN

(2) Islamic Republic of Pakistan

(3) Pākistān

(4) Pakistan is bounded on the northwest by Afghanistan, on the north by the U.S.S.R. and China, on the east by India, and on the south by the Arabian Sea.

(5) Islamabad

(6) Pakistan comprises 33 administrative units; 1 federal capital district (Islamabad), 3 federal northern areas, 4 azad kashmir districts, 4 provinces, and 21 federal tribal areas.

Federal Northern Areas	Capitals
1. Balistan	Skardu
2. Diamir	Chilas
3. Gilgit	Gilgit

Azad Kashmir Districts	Capitals
4. Kotli	Kotli

5. Mirpur	Mirpur
6. Muzaffarabad	Muzaffarabad
7. Punch	Punch

Provinces	Capitals
8. Balúchistán	Quetta
9. North West Frontier	Peshawar
10. Punjab	Lahore
11. Sind	Karachi

Federal Tribal Areas (all administered from Islamabad)
12. Chitral
13. Dir
14. Swat
15. Malakand
16. Amb
17. Hazara
18. Zhob
19. Loralai
20. Dalbandin
21. Marri
22. Bugti
23. Peshawar
24. Kohat
25. Dera Ismail Khan
26. Banu
27. Bajaur
28. Mohmand
29. Khyber
30. Kurram
31. North Waziristan
32. South Waziristan

(1) PANAMA

(2) Republic of Panama

(3) República de Panamá

(4) Panama is bounded on the north by the Caribbean, on the east by Colombia, on the south by the Pacific, and on the west by Costa Rica.

(5) Panama City

(6) Panama comprises 10 administrative units; 1 territory or "co-marca" (San Blas/El Porvenir, capital) and 9 provinces.

Provinces	Capitals
1. Bocas del Toro	Bocas del Toro
2. Chiriquí	David
3. Coclé	Penonomé
4. Colón	Colón
5. Herrera	Chitré
6. Darién	La Palma
7. Panama	Ciudad Panama
8. Veraguas	Santiago
9. Los Santos	Las Tablas

(1) PAPUA NEW GUINEA

(2) Papua New Guinea

(3) Papua New Guinea

(4) Papua New Guinea extends from the equator to the Louisiade Archipelago and from the border of Indonesia's West Irian to 160° east longitude.

(5) Port Moresby

(6) Papua New Guinea comprises 20 administrative units; 1 national capital district (Port Moresby) and 19 provinces.

Provinces	Capitals
1. Milne Bay	Alotau
2. Northern	Popondetta
3. Central	Port Moresby
4. Gulf	Kerema
5. Western	Daru
6. Southern Highlands	Mendi
7. Western Highlands	Mount Hagen
8. Simbu	Kundiawa
9. Eastern Highlands	Goroka
10. Morobe	Lae
11. Madang	Madang
12. East Sepik	Wewak
13. West Sepik	Vanimo
14. Manus	Lorengau
15. West New Britain	Kimbe
16. East New Britain	Rabaul
17. New Ireland	Kavieng
18. North Solomons	Arawa
19. Enga	Webag

(2) The Republic of Paraguay

(3) República del Paraguay

(4) Paraguay is situated in the center of South America, bounded on the east by Brazil, on the south by Argentina, and on the west by Bolivia.

(5) Asunción

(6) Paraguay comprises 17 administrative units; 1 federal capital district (Asunción) and 16 departments.

Departments	Capitals
1. Central	Asunción
2. Caaguazú	Coronel Oveido
3. Paraguarí	Paraguarí
4. Itapua	Encarnación
5. Cordillera	Caapucú
6. San Pedro	San Pedro
7. Guairá	Villarrica
8. Concepción	Concepción
9. Caazapá	Caazapá
10. Alto Paraná	Tacurupucú
11. Neembucu	Pilar
12. Misiones	San Juan Bautista
13. Amambay	Pedro Juan Caballero
14. Presidente Hayes	Villa Hayes
15. Boquerón	Moriscal Estigarriba
16. Olímpo	Fuerte Olímpo

(1) PERU

(2) The Republic of Peru

(3) República del Perú

(4) Peru is located in northwestern South America. It is bounded by Ecuador on the north, by Colombia and Brazil on the northeast and east, by Bolivia on the southeast, by Chile on the south, and by the Pacific Ocean on the west.

(5) Lima

(6) Peru comprises 24 administrative units; 1 constitutional province (Callao) and 23 departments.

Departments	Capitals
1. Amazonas	Chachapoyas
2. Ancash	Huaraz
3. Apurímac	Abancay
4. Arequipa	Arequipa
5. Ayacucho	Ayacucho
6. Cajamarca	Cajamarca
7. Cuzco	Cuzco
8. Huancavelica	Huancavelica
9. Huánuco	Huánuco
10. Ica	Ica
11. Junín	Huancayo
12. La Libertad	Trujillo
13. Lambayeque	Chiclayo
14. Lima	Lima
15. Loreto	Iquitos
16. Madre de Dios	Maldonado
17. Moquegua	Moquegua
18. Pasco	Cerro de Pasco
19. Piura	Piura
20. Puno	Puno
21. San Martín	Moyobamba
22. Tacna	Tacna
23. Tumbes	Tumbes

(1) PHILIPPINES

(2) Republic of the Philippines

(3) Republika ñg Pilipinas

(4) The Philippines is composed of 7,100 islands in the Pacific, situated between 21°25' and 4°23' north latitude and between 116° and 127° east longitude.

(5) Manila

(6) The Philippines comprises 148 administrative units; 73 provinces, 2 subprovinces, 13 regions, and 60 chartered cities.

Provinces	Capitals
1. Batangas	Batangas
2. Ilocos Norte	Laoag
3. Cagayan	Tuguegarao
4. Abra	Bangued
5. Kalinga-Apayao	Tabuk
6. Ilocos Sur	Vigan
7. Mountain	Bontoc

8.	Isabela	Ilagan
9.	Ifugao	Lagawe
10.	La Union	San Fernando
11.	Benguet	La Trinidad
12.	Nueva Vizcaya	Bayombong
13.	Quirino	Cabarroquis
14.	Pangasinan	Lingayen
15.	Nueva Ecija	Palayan
16.	Quezon	Lucena
17.	Zambales	Iba
18.	Tarlac	Tarlac
19.	Pampanga	San Fernando
20.	Bulacan	Malolos
21.	Bataan	Balanga
22.	Rizal	Pasig
23.	Cavite	Trece Matires
24.	Laguna	Santa Cruz
25.	Camarines Norte	Daet
26.	Batanes	Basco
27.	Camarines Sur	Naga
28.	Catanduanes	Virac
29.	Mindoro Occidental	Mamburao
30.	Mindoro Oriental	Calapan
31.	Marinduque	Boac
32.	Albay	Legazpi
33.	Romblon	Romblon
34.	Sorsogon	Sorsogon
35.	Masbate	Masbate
36.	Northern Samar	Catarman
37.	Aklan	Kalibo
38.	Western Samar	Catbalogan
39.	Eastern Samar	Borongan
40.	Capiz	Roxas
41.	Antique	San Jose de Buenavista
42.	Iloilo	Iloilo
43.	Leyte	Tacloban
44.	Cebu	Cebu
45.	Southern Leyte	Maasin
46.	Negros Occidental	Bacolod
47.	Bohol	Tagbilaran
48.	Surigao del Norte	Surigao
49.	Palawan	Puerto Princesa
50.	Negros Oriental	Dumaguete
51.	Siquijor	Siquijor
52.	Agusan del Norte	Butuan
53.	Camiguin	Mambajao
54.	Surigao del Sur	Tandag
55.	Misamis Oriental	Cagayan de Oro
56.	Zamboanga del Norte	Dipolog
57.	Misamis Occidental	Oroquieta
58.	Bukidnon	Malaybalay

		Capitals
59.	Agusan del Sur	Prosperidad
60.	Zamboanga del Sur	Pagadian
61.	Lanao del Norte	Iligan
62.	Lanao del Sur	Marawi
63.	Davao del Norte	Tagum
64.	Davao Oriental	Mati
65.	Maguindanao	Maganoy
66.	North Cotabato	Kidapawan
67.	Basilan	Isabela
68.	Sultan Kudarat	Isulan
69.	Davao del Sur	Digos
70.	South Cotabato	Koronadal
71.	Sulu	Jolo
72.	Tawitawi	Balimbing
73.	Aurora	Aurora

Subprovinces   Capitals

74.	Guimaras	Guimaras
75.	Biliran	Biliran

Regions   Capitals

76.	Ilocos	
77.	Cagayan Valley	
78.	Central Luzon	
79.	Southern Tagalog	
80.	Bicol	
81.	Western Visayas	
82.	Central Visayas	
83.	Eastern Visayas	
84.	Western Mindanao	
85.	Northern Mindanao	
86.	Southern Mindanao	Davao
87.	Central Mindanao	
88.	National Capital/Metro- politan Manila	Manila

Chartered Cities

89.	Baguio
90.	Dagupan
91.	Laoag
92.	San Carlos (Pangasinan Prov.)
93.	Angeles
94.	Cabanatuan
95.	Olongapo
96.	Palayan
97.	San Jose
98.	Batangas
99.	Cavite
100.	Lipa
101.	Lucena
102.	Puerto Princessa

103. San Pablo
104. Tagaytay
105. Trece Martirez
106. Iriga
107. Legaspi
108. Naga
109. Bacolod
110. Bago
111. Cadiz
112. Iloilo
113. La Carlota
114. Roxas
115. San Carlos (Negros Occidental Prov.)
116. Silay
117. Bais
118. Canlaon
119. Cebu
120. Danao
121. Dumaguete
122. Lapulapu
123. Mandaue
124. Tagbilaran
125. Toledo
126. Calbayog
127. Ormoc
128. Dapitan
129. Dipolog
130. Pagadian
131. Zamboanga
132. Butuan
133. Cagayan de Oro
134. Gingoog
135. Oroquieta
136. Ozamis
137. Surigao
138. Tangub
139. Davao
140. General Santos
141. Cotabato
142. Iligan
143. Marawi
144. Caloocan
145. Manila
146. Pasay
147. Quezon
148. Tacloban

(1) PITCAIRN ISLAND

(2) British South Pacific Pitcairn Island

(3) British South Pacific Pitcairn Island

(4) Pitcairn is situated in the Pacific Ocean, nearly equidistant from New Zealand and Panama.

(5) Adamstown

(6) Pitcairn Island is a small island without need for local divisions.

(1) POLAND

(2) The Polish People's Republic

(3) Polska Rzeczpospolita Ludowa

(4) Poland is bounded on the north by the Baltic and the R.S.F.S.R.; on the east by Lithuania, White Russia, and the Ukraine; on the south by Czechoslovakia; and on the west by the German Democratic Republic.

(5) Warsaw

(6) Poland comprises 49 administrative units known as provinces or "województwa."

Województwa	Capitals
1. Warszawskie	Warsaw
2. Bialskopodlaskie	Biala Podlaska
3. Bialostockie	Bialystok
4. Bielskie	Bielsko Biala
5. Bydgoskie	Bydgoszcz
6. Chelmskie	Chelm
7. Ciechanowskie	Ciechanów
8. Czestochowskie	Czestochawa
9. Elblaskie	Elblag
10. Gdańskie	Gdańsk
11. Gorzowskie	Gorzów
12. Jeleniogórskie	Jelenia Góra
13. Kaliskie	Kalisz
14. Katowickie	Katowice
15. Kielce	Kielce
16. Konińskie	Konín
17. Koszalińskie	Koszalin

18. Krakowskie	Kraków
19. Krośnieńskie	Krosno
20. Legnickie	Legnica
21. Leszczyńskie	Leszno
22. Lubelskie	Lublin
23. Lomzyńskie	Lomża
24. Lódzkie	Lodź
25. Nowosadeckie	Nowy Sącz
26. Olsztyńskie	Olsztyn
27. Opolskie	Opole
28. Ostroleckie	Ostroleka
29. Pilskie	Pila
30. Piotrkowskie	Piotrków Trybunalski
31. Plockie	Plock
32. Poznańskie	Poznań
33. Przemyskie	Przemyśl
34. Radomskie	Radom
35. Rzeszowskie	Rzeszów
36. Siedleckie	Siedlce
37. Sieradzkie	Sieradz
38. Skierniewickie	Skierniewickie
39. Slupskie	Slupsk
40. Suwalskie	Suwalskie
41. Szczecinskie	Szczecin
42. Tarnobrzeskie	Tarnobrzeg
43. Tarnowskie	Tarnów
44. Torunskie	Toruń
45. Walbrzyskie	Walbrzych
46. Wloclowskie	Wloclawek
47. Wroclawskie	Wroclaw
48. Zamojskie	Zamość
49. Zielonogórskie	Zielona Góra

(1) PORTUGAL

(2) The Portuguese Republic

(3) República Portuguesa

(4) Portugal lies on the western side of the Iberian Peninsula known as Continental Portugal. Portugal also includes the islands in the Atlantic named the Azores and Madeira.

(5) Lisbon

(6) Portugal comprises 22 administrative units known as districts.

Districts	Capitals
1. Angra do Heroismo	Angra do Heroismo

2.	Aveiro	Aveiro
3.	Beja	Beja
4.	Braga	Braga
5.	Bragança	Bragança
6.	Castelo Branco	Castelo Branco
7.	Coimbra	Coimbra
8.	Évora	Évora
9.	Faro	Faro
10.	Funchal	Funchal
11.	Guarda	Guarda
12.	Horta	Horta
13.	Leiria	Leiria
14.	Lisboa	Lisboa
15.	Ponta Delgado	Ponta Delgado
16.	Portalegre	Portalegre
17.	Oporto	Oporto
18.	Santarém	Santarém
19.	Setúbal	Setúbal
20.	Viano do Castelo	Viano do Castelo
21.	Vila Real	Vila Real
22.	Viseu	Viseu

(1) PUERTO RICO

(2) Commonwealth of Puerto Rico

(3) Commonwealth of Puerto Rico

(4) Puerto Rico is the most easterly island of the Greater Antilles. It lies between the Dominican Republic and the United States Virgin Islands.

(5) San Juan

(6) Puerto Rico comprises 77 administrative units known as "municipales."

Municipales
1. Bayamon
2. Boa Alta
3. Boa Baja
4. Corozal
5. Gurabo
6. Juncos
7. Yabucoa
8. Maunabo
9. Carolina
10. Loiza

11. Rio Grande
12. Luquillo
13. Dorado
14. Barceloneta
15. Hatillo
16. Camuy
17. Guayama
18. Cayey
19. Arroyo
20. Patillas
21. Humacao
22. San Lorenzo
23. Las Piedras
24. Cataño
25. Naranjito
26. Comerioq
27. Barranquitas
28. Orocovis
29. Aibonito
30. Fajardo
31. Naguabo
32. Ceiba
33. Caguas
34. Aguas Buenas
35. Cidra
36. Manati
37. Vega Alta
38. Vega Baja
39. Morovis
40. Ciales
41. Arecibo
42. Utuado
43. Trujillo Alto
44. San Juan
45. Ponce
46. Ponce I
47. Ponce II
48. Adjuntas
49. Jayuya
50. Santa Isabel
51. Salinas
52. Villalba
53. Juana Diaz
54. Coamo
55. Peñuelas
56. Guayanilla
57. Yauco
58. Guanica
59. Mayaguez
60. Maricao
61. Las Marias

```
62.  Hormigueros
63.  Cabo Rojo
64.  San German
65.  Sabana Grande
66.  Lajas
67.  Añasco
68.  Rincon
69.  Moca
70.  San Sebastian
71.  Lares
72.  Aguadilla
73.  Aguada
74.  Isabela
75.  Quebradillas
76.  Vieques
77.  Colebra
```

(1) QATAR

(2) The State of Qatar

(3) Dawlat Qatar

(4) Qatar includes the whole of the Arabian Qatar Peninsula and extends on the landward side from Khor al Odeid to the boundaries of the Saudi Arabian Hasa Province.

(5) Doha

(6) Qatar comprises 6 administrative units known as municipal councils.

Municipal Councils
1. Doha
2. Dikhan
3. Umm Said
4. Al Khawr
5. Zubarah
6. Umm Bab

(1) RÉUNION

(2) French Overseas Department of Réunion

(3) Île de la Réunion Département Outremer

(4) Réunion is an island located about 569 miles east of Madagascar.

(5) Saint-Denis

(6) Réunion comprises 26 administrative units; 2 arrondissements and 24 communes.

Arrondissements	Capitals
1. Du Vent	St-Denis
2. Sous le Vent	St. Pierre

Communes
3. Bras-Panon
4. Cilaos
5. Entre-Deux
6. La Plaines-des-Palmistes
7. La Possession
8. Le Port
9. Les Avirons
10. Les Trois-Bassins
11. Le Tempon
12. L-Étang-Salé
13. Petite-Île
14. Sainte-Marie
15. Sainte-Rose
16. Sainte-Suzanne
17. Salazie
18. Saint-André
19. Saint-Benoit
20. Saint-Denis
21. Saint-Joseph
22. Saint-Leu
23. Saint-Louis
24. Saint-Paul
25. Saint-Philippe
26. Saint-Pierre

(1)   ROMANIA

(2) The Socialist Republic of Romania

(3) Republica Socialistă România

(4) Romania is located in eastcentral Europe. It is bounded by the U.S.S.R. on the north, by the U.S.S.R. and the Black Sea on the east, by Bulgaria on the south, and by Yugoslavia and Hungary on the west.

(5) Bucharest

(6) Romania comprises 40 administrative units known as districts.

Districts	Capitals
1. Alba	Alba Iulia
2. Arad	Arad
3. Arges	Piteşti
4. Bacău	Bacău
5. Bihor	Oradea
6. Bistriţa-Nasaud	Bistriţa
7. Botoşani	Botoşani
8. Braşov	Braşov
9. Brăila	Brăila
10. Buzău	Buzău
11. Caraş-Severin	Reşita
12. Cluj	Cluj-Napoca
13. Constanţa	Constanţa
14. Covasna	St. Gheorghe
15. Dîmbovita	Tîrgovişte
16. Dolj	Craiova
17. Galaţi	Galaţi
18. Gorj	Tbrgu Jiu
19. Harghita	Miercurea Ciuc
20. Hunedoara	Deva
21. Ialomiţa	Slobozia
22. Iaşi	Iaşi
23. Ilfov	Bucarest
24. Maramureş	Baia Mare
25. Mehedinţi	Drobeta-Turnu-Severin
26. Mureş	Tirgu Mures
27. Neamţ	Piatra Neamt
28. Olt	Slatina
29. Prahova	Ploieşti
30. Satu Mare	Satu Mare
31. Sălaj	Zalău
32. Sibiu	Sibiu
33. Suceava	Suceava
34. Teleorman	Alexandra
35. Timiş	Timişoara
36. Tulcea	Tulcea
37. Vaslui	Vaslui
38. Vîlcea	Rimnicu Vîlcea
39. Vrancea	Focşani
40. Bucharest	Bucharest

(1) RWANDA

(2) The Republic of Rwanda

(3) République du Rwanda

136

(4) Rwanda is bounded on the south by Burundi, on the west by Lake Kivu and the Congo, on the north by Uganda, and on the east by Tanzania.

(5) Kigali

(6) Rwanda comprises 10 administrative units known as prefectures.

Prefectures	Capitals
1. Kigali	Kigali
2. Kibungo	Kibungo
3. Byumba	Byumba
4. Ruhengeri	Ruhengeri
5. Gisenyi	Gisenyi
6. Kibuye	Kibuye
7. Gitarama	Gitarama
8. Gikongoro	Gikongoro
9. Butare	Butare
10. Cyangugu	Cyangugu

(1) ST. HELENA

(2) British Colony of St. Helena

(3) British Colony of St. Helena

(4) St. Helena is an island of volcanic origin 1,200 miles from the west coast of Africa.

(5) Jamestown

(6) St. Helena comprises 11 administrative units; 3 island councils and 8 districts.

Councils
1. St. Helena
2. Ascensin
3. Tristan da Cunha

Districts
4. Blue Hill
5. Half Tree Hollow
6. Levelwood
7. Longwood
8. Lower Jamestown
9. Upper Jamestown
10. St. Paul's
11. Sandy Bay

137

(1)   ST. KITTS AND NEVIS

(2)   Associated State of St. Kitts-Nevis

(3)   Associated State of St. Kitts-Nevis

(4)   St. Kitts and Nevis are islands in the eastern Caribbean's
      West Indies.

(5)   Basseterre

(6)   St. Kitts and Nevis comprises 14 administrative units known as
      parishes.

Parishes	Capitals
1. St. Paul	Capisterre
2. St. Anne	Sandy Point
3. St. Thomas	Middle Island
4. Trinity	Palmetto Point
5. St. George	Basseterre
6. St. Peter	Basseterre
7. St. Mary	Cayon
8. Christ Church	Nicholas Town
9. St. John	Capisterre
10. St. Thomas (Nevis)	Cotton Ground
11. St. Paul (Nevis)	Charlestown
12. St. John (Nevis)	Figtree
13. St. George (Nevis)	Gingerland
14. St. James (Nevis)	Windward

(1)   ST. LUCIA

(2)   St. Lucia

(3)   St. Lucia

(4)   St. Lucia is a small island of the Lesser Antilles. It is 238
      square miles in area, and it is located in the eastern Carib-
      bean.

(5)   Castries

(6)   St. Lucia comprises 10 administrative units known as local
      government councils.

Local Government Councils
1.   Castries

        2. Anse la Raye
        3. Canaries
        4. Choiseul
        5. Dennery
        6. Gros Islet
        7. La Borie
        8. Micoud
        9. Soufriere
        10. Vieux Fort

(1) ST. PIERRE AND MIQUELON

(2) French Overseas Department of St. Pierre and Miquelon

(3) Département d'Outremer des Îles Saint-Pierre-et-Miquelon

(4) St. Pierre and Miquelon Islands lie about 25 kilometers from
the coast of Newfoundland, Canada in the Atlantic Ocean.

(5) St. Pierre

(6) St. Pierre and Miquelon comprise 2 administrative units known
as communes.

Communes	Capitals
1. St. Pierre	St. Pierre
2. Miquelon	Miquelon

(1) ST. VINCENT AND THE GRENADINES

(2) St. Vincent and The Grenadines

(3) St. Vincent and The Grenadines

(4) St. Vincent is one of the Windward Islands, situated approximately 100 miles west of Barbados in the West Indies. The
nearest neighboring countries are St. Lucia to the north, and
Grenada to the south.

(5) Kingstown

(6) St. Vincent and the Grenadines comprise 6 administrative units;
5 parishes and 1 dependency (The Grenadines/Bequia, capital).

Parishes	Capitals
1. St. David	Chateaubelair

2. Charlotte	Georgetown
3. St. George	Kingstown
4. St. Andrew	Chauncey
5. St. Patrick	Barrovallie

(1) SAN MARINO

(2) Republic of San Marino

(3) Repubblica di San Marino

(4) San Marino is a landlocked state in central Italy, 20 kilometers from the Adriatic Sea.

(5) San Marino City

(6) San Marino comprises 10 administrative units known as sectors or "castelli."

Castelli	Capitals
1. Aquaviva	Aquaviva
2. Borgo	Borgo
3. Chiesanuova	Chiesanuova
4. Domagnano	Domagnano
5. Faetano	Faetano
6. Fiorentino	Fiorentino
7. La Pleve	La Pleve
8. Montegiardino	Montegiardino
9. Sarravalle	Sarravalle
10. San Giovanni	San Giovanni

(1) SAÕ TOMÉ AND PRINCIPE

(2) Democratic Republic of Saõ Tomé and Príncipe.

(3) República de Saõ Tomé e Príncipe

(4) The islands of Saõ Tomé and Príncipe lie 125 miles off the coast of Africa, in the Gulf of Guinea.

(5) Saõ Tomé City

(6) Saõ Tomé and Príncipe comrpises 2 administrative units known as provinces.

Provinces	Capitals
1. Saõ Tomé	Saõ Tomé City
2. Principe	Principe

(1) SAUDI ARABIA

(2) The Saudi Arabian Kingdom

(3) Al-Mamlaka al-^{C}Arabiya as-Sa^{C}udiya

(4) Saudi Arabia occupies about four-fifths of the Arabian Peninsula, with North Yemen and the Red Sea to the west, and
the Persian Gulf and the U.A.E. to the east. Jordan, Iraq,
and Kuwait are to the north, and Oman and South Yemen are
to the south.

(5) Riyadh

(6) Saudi Arabia comprises 18 administrative units known as
provinces.

Provinces	Capitals
1. Qurayyat	Kaf
2. Northern	Wejh
3. Al-Jawf	Al-Jawf
4. Northern Frontiers	Nisab
5. Medinah	Medinah
6. Ha'il	Ha'il
7. Qassim	Buraida
8. Afif	Afif
9. Riyadh	Riyadh
10. Makkah (Mecca)	Makkah (Mecca)
11. Bishah	Qal ^{C}at Bishah
12. Asir	Abha
13. Qisan	Qisan
14. Najran	Najran
15. Eastern	Al Hufuf
16. Khasirah	Khasirah
17. Ranyah	Ranyah
18. Al-Bahah	Al-Bahah

(1) SENEGAL

(2) Republic of Senegal

(3) République du Sénégal

(4) Senegal lies on the west coast of Africa, bordered to the north by Mauritania, to the east by Mali, and to the south by Guinea and Guinea-Bissau. In the southern part The Gambia forms a narrow enclave extending some 200 miles inland.

(5) Dakar

(6) Senegal comprises 36 administrative units; 8 régions and 28 départments.

Régions	Capitals
1. Dakar	Dakar
2. Cassamance	Ziguinchor
3. Valée du Fleuve	St-Louis
4. Thiès	Thiès
5. Diourbel	Diourbel
6. Sine-Saloum	Kaolack
7. Sénégal Oriental	Tambacounda
8. Cap-Vert	Rufisque

Départments	Capitals
9. Thies	Thies
10. Tivaouane	Tivaouane
11. M'Bour	M'Bour
12. Diourbel	Diourbel
13. Bambey	Bambey
14. M'Backe	M'Backe
15. Kaolack	Kaolack
16. Kaffrine	Kaffrine
17. Gossas	Gossas
18. Fatick	Fatick
19. Foundiougne	Foundiougne
20. Nioro	Nioro
21. Ziguinchor	Ziguinchor
22. Sedhiou	Sedhiou
23. Kolda	Kolda
24. Vélingara	Vélingara
25. Oussouye	Oussouye
26. Bignona	Bignona
27. Tambacounda	Tambacounda
28. Kédougou	Kédougou
29. Bakel	Bakel
30. St. Louis	St. Louis
31. Dagana	Dagana
32. Podor	Podor
33. Matam	Matam
34. Louga	Louga
35. Kébémer	Kébémer
36. Linguère	Linguère

(1) SEYCHELLES

(2) The Republic of Seychelles

(3) The Republic of Seychelles

(4) Seychelles comprises 92 islands widely scattered over the western Indian Ocean. The southernmost of the islands are about 209 kilometers north of Madagascar.

(5) Victoria, Mahé Island

(6) Seychelles comprises 10 administrative units known as island councils.

<u>Island Councils</u>
1. Mahé (Victoria)
2. Praslin
3. La Digue
4. Silhouette
5. Curieuse
6. Felicité
7. Frigate
8. Bird
9. Cousin
10. Cousine

(1) SIERRA LEONE

(2) The Republic of Sierra Leone

(3) The Republic of Sierra Leone

(4) Sierra Leone is bounded on the northwest, north, and northeast by the Republic of Guinea; on the southeast by Liberia; and on the southwest by the Atlantic Ocean.

(5) Freetown

(6) Sierra Leone comprises 4 administrative units; 1 special area (Western/Freetown, capital) and 3 provinces.

Provinces	Capitals
1. Northern	Makeni
2. Eastern	Kenema
3. Southern	Bo

(1)   SINGAPORE

(2)   The Republic of Singapore

(3)   The Republic of Singapore

(4)   Singapore Island is situated off the southern extremity of the
      Malay peninsula, with the body of water separating it from
      the mainland being the Straits of Johore.

(5)   Singapore City

(6)   Singapore comprises 71 administrative units known as parlia-
      mentary constituencies, each having its own Citizens Consul-
      tative Committees.

Parliamentary Constituencies
1. Kallang
2. Sembawang
3. Bukit Merah
4. Brickwords
5. Braddell Heights
6. Kim Seng
7. River Valley
8. Kampong Chai Chee
9. Cairnhill
10. Bedok
11. Cheng San
12. Jalan Kayu
13. Tampines
14. Aljunied
15. Bukit Panjang
16. Tiong Bahru
17. Kolam Ayer
18. Jurong
19. Mountbatten
20. Changi
21. Kompong Ubi
22. Rochore
23. Jalan Besar
24. Bukit Timah
25. Siglap
26. Khe Bong
27. Queenstown
28. Punggol
29. Paya Lebar
30. Chu Chu Kang
31. Kuo Chuan
32. Toa Payoh
33. Katong

34. Bukit Ho Swee
35. Tanah Merah
36. Moulmein
37. Whampoa
38. Delta
39. Ulu Pandan
40. Ang Mo Kio
41. Buona Vista
42. Bukit Batok
43. Henderson
44. Serangoon Gardens
45. Leng Kee
46. Kampong Kembangan
47. Alexandro
48. Clementi
49. Nee Soon
50. Telok Blangah
51. Chong Boon
52. Thomson
53. Pasir Panjang
54. Boon Lay
55. Radin Mas
56. Yio Chu Kang
57. Boon Teck
58. Geylang Serai
59. Kaki Bukit
60. Ayer Rajah
61. West Coast
62. Anson
63. Kreta Ayer
64. Kampong Glam
65. Havelock
66. Telok Ayer
67. Tanglin
68. MacPherson
69. Kim Keat
70. Potong Pasir
71. Geylang West

(1) SOLOMON ISLANDS

(2) Independent State of Solomon Islands

(3) Independent State of Solomon Islands

(4) The Solomon Islands lie in the Pacific within the area 5° to 12°30' south latitude and 155°30' to 169°45' east longitude.

(5) Honiara

145

(6)   Solomon Islands comprise 8 administrative units known as local government area councils.

Local Government Area Councils	Capitals
1. Central Islands	Honiara
2. Eastern Islands (Temotu)	Graciosa Bay
3. Western	Gizo
4. Guadalcanal	Honiara
5. Honiara	Honiara
6. Makira-Ulawa	Kira Kira
7. Malaita	Auki
8. Santa Isabel	Buala

(1)   SOMALIA

(2)   Somali Democratic Republic

(3)   Al-Jumhouriya As-Soomaaliya Al-Domocradia

(4)   Somalia lies on the east coast of Africa, with Ethiopia to the northwest, Kenya to the west, and with a short frontier with Djibouti.

(5)   Mogadishu

(6)   Somalia comprises 16 administrative units known as regions.

Regions	Capitals
1. Jubbada Hoose	Chisimayu
2. Jubbada Dhexe	Bu'aale
3. Shabellaha Hoose	Merca
4. Banadir	Mogadishu
5. Shabellaha Dhexe	Giohar
6. Bay	Baidoa
7. Gedo	Garbahaarrey
8. Bakool	Oddur
9. Hiiraan	Beled Weyne
10. Galguduud	Dusa Marreb
11. Mudug	Galcaio
12. Nugaal	Garoe
13. Bari	Bender Cassim
14. Sanaag	Ceerigaabo
15. Togdheer	Burao
16. Woqooyi Galbeed	Hargeysa

(1) SOUTH AFRICA

(2) The Republic of South Africa

(3) Republiek van Suid-Afrika

(4) South Africa is bounded on the north by Namibia, Botswana, and Zimbabwe; on the northeast by Mozambique and Swaziland; on the east by the Indian Ocean; and on the south and west by the south Atlantic.

(5) Pretoria

(6) South Africa comprises 15 administrative units; 4 provinces, 4 independent republics, 6 national states and 1 external territory (Walvis Bay/Walvis Bay, capital).

Provinces	Capitals
1. Cape	Cape Town
2. Orange Free State	Bloemfontein
3. Transvaal	Pretoria
4. Natal	Pietermaritzburg

Independent Republics	Capitals
5. Transkei	Umtata
6. Venda	Thohoyandou
7. Bophuthatswana	Mmabatho
8. Ciskei	Zwelitsha

National States	Capitals
9. Kwa Zulu	Ulundi
10. Qwaqwa	Phuthaditjhaba
11. Lebowa	Lebowakgomo
12. Gazankulu	Giyani
13. Ka Ngwane	Louieville
14. Kwa Ndebele	Siyabuswa

(1) SOUTH KOREA

(2) Republic of Korea

(3) Taehan-Min'guk

(4) South Korea forms the southern part of the Korean Peninsula between north China and Japan. To the north is North Korea, separated by a frontier which roughly follows the 38th parallel.

(5) Seoul

(6) South Korea comprises 11 administrative units; 2 special municipalities and 9 provinces.

Special Municipalities
1. Seoul
2. Pusan

Provinces	Capitals
3. Kyonngi	Suwon
4. Kangwon	Chuchon
5. Chungbuk	Chongju
6. Chungnam	Taejon
7. Chonbuk	Chonju
8. Chonnam	Kwangju
9. Kyongbuk	Taegu
10. Kyongnam	Pusan
11. Cheju	Cheju

(1) SOUTH YEMEN

(2) The People's Democratic Republic of Yemen

(3) Al-Yaman ash-Sha^{c}btyah

(4) South Yemen lies on the southern shore of the Arabian Peninsula, with North Yemen to the northwest, Saudi Arabia to the north, and Oman to the east. The islands of Perim and Kamaran at the southern end of the Red Sea are part of South Yemen.

(5) Madanal Al-Sha'ab al-Ittihad (Aden)

(6) South Yemen comprises 6 administrative units known as governorates or "muhāfazat."

Muhāfazat	Capitals
1. Hadramawt	Mukalla
2. Shabwah	Shabwah
3. Al Ghaydah	Al Ghaydah
4. Abyan	Abyan
5. Tuban	Tuban
6. ^{c}Adan	^{c}Adan

(1) SPAIN

(2) The Spanish State

148

(3)　Estado Español

(4)　Spain is bounded on the north by the Bay of Biscay and the
　　　Pyrenees (forming the French frontier); on the east and south
　　　by the Mediterranean and the Straits of Gibraltar; on the
　　　southwest by the Atlantic; and on the west by Portugal and
　　　the Atlantic.

(5)　Madrid

(6)　Spain comprises 45 administrative units; 3 African enclaves,
　　　2 African presidios, and 40 provinces.

African Enclaves
　1.　Alhucemas
　2.　Chafarinas
　3.　Peñon de Vélez

African Presidios	Capitals
4. Ceuta	Ceuta
5. Melilla	Melilla

Provinces	Capitals
6. Cádiz	Cádiz
7. Castellón	Castellón
8. Ciudad-Real	Ciudad-Real
9. Córdoba	Córdoba
10. La Coruña	La Coruña
11. Cuenca	Cuenca
12. Gerona	Gerona
13. Grenada	Grenada
14. Guadalajara	Guadalajara
15. Guinpúzcoa	San Sebastian
16. Huelva	Huelva
17. Huesca	Huesca
18. Jaén	Jaén
19. León	León
20. Lérida	Lérida
21. Longroño	Longroño
22. Lugo	Lugo
23. Madrid	Madrid
24. Málaga	Málaga
25. Murcia	Murcia
26. Navarra	Pamplona
27. Orense	Orense
28. Oviedo	Oviedo
29. Palencia	Palencia
30. Las Palmas	Las Palmas
31. Pontevedra	Pontevedra
32. Salamanca	Salamanca
33. Santa Cruz de Tenerife	Santa Cruz de Tenerife

34.	Santandar	Santandar
35.	Segovia	Segovia
36.	Sevilla	Sevilla
37.	Soria	Soria
38.	Tarragona	Tarragona
39.	Teruel	Teruel
40.	Toledo	Toledo
41.	Valencia	Valencia
42.	Valladolid	Valladolid
43.	Viscaya	Viscaya
44.	Zamora	Zamora
45.	Zaragoza	Zaragoza

(1) SRI LANKA

(2) Republic of Sri Lanka

(3) Republic of Sri Lanka

(4) Sri Lanka lies off the southeast coast of the Indian State of Tamil Nadu, separated from it by the Indian Ocean.

(5) Colombo

(6) Sri Lanka comprises 22 administrative units known as districts.

Districts	Capitals
1. Amparai	Amparai
2. Anuradhapura	Anuradhapura
3. Badulla	Badulla
4. Batticaloa	Batticaloa
5. Colombo	Colombo
6. Galle	Galle
7. Hambantota	Hambantota
8. Jaffna	Jaffna
9. Kalutara	Kalutara
10. Kandy	Kandy
11. Kegalla	Kegalla
12. Kurunegala	Kurunegala
13. Mannar	Mannar
14. Matale	Matale
15. Matara	Matara
16. Monaragalla	Monaragalla
17. Nuwara Eliya	Nuwara Eliya
18. Polonnaruwa	Polonnaruwa
19. Puttalam	Puttalam
20. Ratnapura	Ratnapura
21. Trincomalee	Trincomalee
22. Vavuniya	Vavuniya

(1) SUDAN

(2) Democratic Republic of the Sudan

(3) Jamhuryat es-Sudan Al Democratia

(4) Sudan lies in northeast Africa. To the north is Egypt, to the east is Ethiopia and the Red Sea, to the west the Central African Republic and Chad, and to the south are Kenya, Uganda, and Zaïre.

(5) Khartoum

(6) Sudan comprises 21 administrative units; 1 national capital district (Khartoum), 6 regions, and 14 provinces.

Regions	Capitals
1. Central	Wad Madani
2. Northern	Ad Damir
3. Eastern	Kassala
4. Kordofan	Al Ubayyid
5. Darfur	Al Fashir
6. Southern	Juba

Provinces	Capitals
7. Ash Shamālīyah	Dunquiah
8. An Nil	Ad Dâmir
9. Al Bahr Al Ahmar	Port Sudan
10. Al Khurtūm	Khurtūm
11. Kassalā	Kassalā
12. An Nil Al Azraq	Ad Damazin
13. A Ali an Nil	Malakāl
14. Junqali	Bor
15. Al Istiwā-Īyahal Ash Sharqīyah	Juba
16. Al Istiwā-Īyahal Al Gharbīyah	Yambio
17. Al Buhayrah	Rumbek
18. Bahr Al Ghazal	Wâw
19. Dārfūr Al Janūbīyah	Nyala
20. Dārfūr Ash Shamālīyah	Al Fāshir

(1) SURINAM

(2) Republic of Surinam

(3) Republiek van Suriname

(4) Surinam is situated on the north coast of South America and is bounded on the north by the Atlantic Ocean; on the east by the Marowijne River, which separates it from French Guiana; on the west by Guyana; and on the south by Brazil.

(5) Paramaribo

(6) Surinam comprises 8 administrative units; 1 capital district (Paramaribo), and 7 districts.

Districts	Capitals
1. Brokopondo	Brokopondo
2. Commewijne	Nieuw Amsterdam
3. Coronie	Totness
4. Marowijne	Albina
5. Nickerie	Nieuw Nickerie
6. Saramacca	Groningen
7. Suriname	Paramaribo

(1) SVALBARD

(2) Svalbard

(3) Svalbard

(4) Svalbard is an archipelago in the Arctic situated between 10° and 35° east longitude and between 74° and 81° north latitude.

(5) Longyearbyen

(6) Svalbard comprises 5 administrative units known as government meterological stations.

Stations
1. Longyearben
2. Bjørnøya
3. Hopen
4. Isfjord
5. Ny-Ålesund

(1) SWAZILAND

(2) The Kingdom of Swaziland

(3) The Kingdom of Swaziland

(4) Swaziland is bounded on the north, west, and south by South Africa.

(5) Mbabane

(6) Swaziland comprises 4 administrative districts.

Districts	Capitals
1. Shiselweni	Nhlangano
2. Lubombo	Siteki
3. Manzini	Manzini
4. Hhohho	Mbabane

(1) SWEDEN

(2) The Kingdom of Sweden

(3) Konungariket Sverige

(4) Sweden is located in northwestern Europe. It is bounded by Norway on the west and north; by Finland, the Gulf of Bothnia and the Baltic Sea on the east; and by Denmark on the southwest.

(5) Stockholm

(6) Sweden comprises 24 administrative units known as counties.

Counties	Capitals
1. Stockholm	Stockholm
2. Uppsala	Uppsala
3. Södermanland	Nykoping
4. Östergötland	Linkoping
5. Jönköping	Jönköping
6. Kronoberg	Vaxjo
7. Kalmar	Kalmar
8. Gotland	Visby
9. Blekinge	Karlskrona
10. Kristianstad	Kristianstad
11. Malmöhus	Malmo
12. Halland	Halmstad
13. Göteborg och Bohus	Göteborg
14. Alvsborg	Vanersborg
15. Skaraborg	Mariestad
16. Värmland	Karlstad
17. Örebro	Örebro
18. Västmanland	Vasteras
19. Kopparberg	Falun

20.	Gävleborg	Gavle
21.	Västernorrland	Harnosand
22.	Jämtland	Ostersund
23.	Västerbotten	Umea
24.	Norrbotten	Lulea

(1) SWITZERLAND

(2) The Swiss Confederation

(3) Suisse

(4) Switzerland is located in Central Europe. It is bounded by France on the west, by West Germany on the north, by Austria and Italy on the east, and by Italy on the south.

(5) Bern

(6) Switzerland comprises 26 administrative units known as cantons.

Cantons		Capitals
1.	Zurich	Zurich
2.	Bern	Bern
3.	Luzern	Luzern
4.	Uri	Altdorf
5.	Schwyz	Schwyz
6.	Obwalden	Sarnen
7.	Nidwalden	Stans
8.	Zug	Zug
9.	Glarus	Glarus
10.	Fribourg	Fribourg
11.	Solothurn	Solothurn
12.	Basel-Stadt	Basel
13.	Basel-Land	Liestal
14.	Schaffhausen	Schaffhausen
15.	Ausser-Rhoden	Herisau
16.	Inner-Rhoden	Appenzell
17.	St. Gallen	St. Gallen
18.	Graubunden	Chur
19.	Aargau	Aargau
20.	Thurgau	Trauenfeld
21.	Ticino	Bellinzona
22.	Vaud	Lausanne
23.	Valais	Sion
24.	Neuchatel	Neuchatel
25.	Geneve	Geneve
26.	Jura	Delemont

(1) SYRIA

(2) The Syrian Arab Republic

(3) As-Surīyah

(4) Syria lies on the eastern shore of the Mediterranean Sea, with Turkey to the north, Iraq to the east, and Jordan to the south. Lebanon and Israel are to the southeast.

(5) Damascus

(6) Syria comprises 13 administrative units; 1 independent municipality (Damascus City), and 12 provinces or "mohafazats."

Mohafazats	Capitals
1. El Ladhiqiya	El Ladhiqiya
2. Hama	Hama
3. Idlib	Idlib
4. Aleppo	Aleppo
5. El Rashid	El Rashid
6. Deir-ez-Zor	Deir-ez-Zor
7. Homs	Homs
8. Damascus	Damascus
9. Es Suweida	Es Suweida
10. El Quneitra	El Quneitra
11. Dera^{c}a	Dera^{c}a
12. Haseke	Haseke

(1) TANZANIA

(2) The United Republic of Tanzania

(3) Jamhuri ya Muungano wa Tanzania

(4) Tanzania consists of Tankanyika on the east coast of Africa and the islands of Zanzibar and Pemba. Uganda and Kenya are to the north; Zaïre to the west; and Zambia, Malawi, and Mozambique to the south.

(5) Dar es Salaam

(6) Tanzania comprises 24 administrative units known as regions.

Regions	Capitals
1. Dar es Salaam	Dar es Salaam
2. Mwanza	Mwanza

3.	Kilimanjaro	Moshi
4.	Tanga	Tanga
5.	Mara	Musoma
6.	West Lake	Bukoba
7.	Shinyanga	Shinyanga
8.	Dodoma	Dodoma
9.	Coast	Dar es Salaam
10.	Kigoma	Kigoma
11.	Mtwara	Mtwara
12.	Iringa	Iringa
13.	Mbeya	Mbeya
14.	Morogoro	Morogoro
15.	Singida	Singida
16.	Arusha	Arusha
17.	Ruvuma	Songea
18.	Tabora	Tabora
19.	Lindi	Lindi
20.	Kaskazini	Mkokotoni
21.	Njini	Zanzibar
22.	Kusini	Koani
23.	Pemba	Wete
24.	Rukwa	Mpanda

(1)   THAILAND

(2)   The Kingdom of Thailand

(3)   Prathet Thai

(4)   Thailand is situated in Southeast Asia. It extends far south down the narrow Kra Peninsula to Malaya. It is bordered to the west and north by Burma, to the northeast by Laos, and to the southeast by Kampuchea.

(5)   Bangkok

(6)   Thailand comprises 72 administrative units known as provinces.

Provinces		Capitals
1.	Bangkok	Bangkok
2.	Phranakhorn	Phranakhorn
3.	Thonburi	Thonburi
4.	Nonthaburi	Nonthaburi
5.	Pathumthani	Pathumthani
6.	Kanchanaburi	Kanchanaburi
7.	Nakhornpathom	Nakhornpathom
8.	Ratburi	Ratburi
9.	Phetburi	Phetburi

10.	Singhburi	Singhburi
11.	Chonburi	Chonburi
12.	Chanthaburi	Chanthaburi
13.	Chai-nat	Chai-nat
14.	Prachuapkirikhan	Prachuapkirikhan
15.	Cha-choengsao	Cha-choengsao
16.	Samutsakhorn	Samutsakhorn
17.	Samutsongkhram	Samutsongkhram
18.	Samutjsrakan	Samutjsrakan
19.	Lopburi	Lopburi
20.	Suphanburi	Suphanburi
21.	Phranakhornsri-ayuthaya	Phranakhornsri-ayuthaya
22.	Angthong	Angthong
23.	Nakhornayok	Nakhornayok
24.	Trat	Trat
25.	Saraburi	Saraburi
26.	Prachinburi	Prachinburi
27.	Rayong	Rayong
28.	Kalasin	Kalasin
29.	Khon-kaen	Khon-kaen
30.	Chayaphum	Chayaphum
31.	Nakhornphanom	Nakhornphanom
32.	Nakhornratchsima	Nakhornratchsima
33.	Nongkhai	Nongkhai
34.	Buriram	Buriram
35.	Mahasarakham	Mahasarakham
36.	Roi-et	Roi-et
37.	Loei	Loei
38.	Srisaket	Srisaket
39.	Sakonnakhorn	Sakonnakhorn
40.	Surin	Surin
41.	Ubonratch-thani	Ubonratch-thani
42.	Udornthani	Udornthani
43.	Chumphorn	Chumphorn
44.	Ranong	Ranong
45.	Suratthani	Suratthani
46.	Phang-nga	Phang-nga
47.	Nakhornsrithamrat	Nakhornsrithamrat
48.	Phuket	Phuket
49.	Krabi	Krabi
50.	Phatalung	Phatalung
51.	Trang	Trang
52.	Satun	Satun
53.	Songkhla	Songkhla
54.	Pattani	Pattani
55.	Yala	Yala
56.	Nara-thiwat	Nara-thiwat
57.	Kamphaengphet	Kamphaengphet
58.	Chiengrai	Chiengrai
59.	Chiengmai	Chiengmai
60.	Tak	Tak

61.	Nakhornsawan	Nakhornsawan
62.	Nan	Nan
63.	Phichit	Phichit
64.	Phitsnulok	Phitsnulok
65.	Phetchbun	Phetchbun
66.	Phrae	Phrae
67.	Maehongson	Maehongson
68.	Lampang	Lampang
69.	Lamphun	Lamphun
70.	Sukho-thai	Sukho-thai
71.	Uttaradit	Uttaradit
72.	Uthai-thani	Uthai-thani

(1) TOGO

(2) The Togolese Republic

(3) République du Togo

(4) Togo lies between Benin and Ghana, on the coast of West Africa. It forms a narrow strip stretching north to Upper Volta with Ghana to the west and Benin to the east.

(5) Lomé

(6) Togo comprises 24 administrative districts; 5 régions and 19 districts or "cirçonscriptions."

Régions	Capitals
1. Centrale	Sokodé
2. De la Kara	Lama-Kara
3. Des Plateaux	Atakpamé
4. Des Savanes	Dapaon
5. Maritîme	Lomé

Cirçonscriptions	Capitals
6. Lomé	Lomé
7. Tsévié	Tsévié
8. Anécho	Anécho
9. Atakpamé	Atakpamé
10. Sokodé	Sokodé
11. Lama-Kara	Lama-Kara
12. Bassari	Bassari
13. Mango	Mango
14. Dapango	Dapango
15. Tabligbo	Tabligbo
16. Akposso	Amlamé
17. Klouto	Kpalimé

18. Nautja	Nautja
19. Bafilo	Bafilo
20. Niamtougou	Niamtougou
21. Pagouda	Pagouda
22. Kandé	Kandé
23. Sotouboua	Boutouboua
24. Vogan	Vogan

(1)   TOKELAU

(2)   New Zealand's Associated Territory of Tokelau

(3)   New Zealand's Associated Territory of Tokelau

(4)   Tokelau's three atolls lie 480 kilometers north of Western Samoa in the Pacific Ocean.

(5)   Fenuafala

(6)   Tokelau comprises 3 administrative units known as atoll councils.

<u>Atoll Councils</u>
1.   Atafu
2.   Fakaofo
3.   Nukunonu

(1)   TONGA

(2)   The Kingdom of Tonga

(3)   Pule'anga Fakatu'i ^{c}o Tonga

(4)   Tonga comprises 171 islands in the southwest Pacific, about 400 miles east of Fiji.

(5)   Nuku'alofa, Tongatapu Island

(6)   Tonga comprises 3 administrative districts.

Districts	Capitals
1. Tongatapu	Nuku'alofa
2. Ha'apai	Pangai
3. Vava'u	Neiafu

(1) TORRES STRAIGHT ISLANDS

(2) Torres Straight Islands

(3) Torres Straight Islands

(4) These 70 islands lie between 11° south latitude and the Papua New Guinea mainland. They extend from 141°-144° east longitude.

(5) Thursday Island

(6) Torres Straight Islands comprise 20 administrative units; 3 districts and 17 village councils.

> Districts
> 1. Western
> 2. Eastern
> 3. Central
>
> Village Councils
> 4. Thursday Island
> 5. Hammond Island
> 6. Boigu Island
> 7. Yorke Island
> 8. Moa Island
> 9. Saibai Island
> 10. Badu Island
> 11. Murray Island
> 12. Coconut Island
> 13. Prince of Wales Island
> 14. Stephen Island
> 15. Mabuiag Island
> 16. Warraber Island
> 17. Dauan Island
> 18. Darnley Island
> 19. Yam Island
> 20. Weipa Island

(1) TRINIDAD AND TOBAGO

(2) Republic of Trinidad and Tobago

(3) Republic of Trinidad and Tobago

(4) The island of Trinidad lies 7 miles to the eastward of Venezuela, and is separated from South America by the Gulf of Paria.

(5) Port-of-Spain

(6) Trinidad and Tobago comprise 10 administrative units; 3 special
     municipalities and 7 counties.

Special Municipalities
1. Port-of-Spain
2. San Fernando
3. Arima

Counties	Capitals
4. St. George	Port-of-Spain
5. St. David/St. Andrew	Sangre Grande
6. Nariva-Mayuro	Rio Claro
7. Caroni	Chaguanos
8. Victoria	Princess Town
9. St. Patrick	Siparia
10. Tobago	Scarborough

(1) TRUST TERRITORY OF THE PACIFIC ISLANDS

(2) Trust Territory of the Pacific Islands

(3) Trust Territory of the Pacific Islands

(4) T.T.P.I. consists of 2,125 Western Pacific islands in both the
     Caroline and Marshall Island groups, in an area known as
     Micronesia.

(5) Chala Kanoa, Saipan Island

(6) Trust Territory of the Pacific Islands comprises 6 administrative
     units known as districts.

Districts	Capitals
1. Truk	Moen
2. Marshalls	Majuro
3. Pelau	Koror
4. Yap	Yap Town
5. Ponape	Colonia
6. Marianas	Saipan

(1) TUNISIA

(2) The Republic of Tunisia

161

(3) République de Tunisie

(4) Tunisia lies on the Mediterranean coast of Africa, bordered by Algeria to the west and Libya to the east.

(5) Tunis

(6) Tunisia comprises 18 administrative units known as governorates.

Governorates	Capitals
1. Tunis-Sud	Tunis
2. Tunis	Tunis
3. Banzart	Banzart
4. Bajah	Bajah
5. Jundubah	Jundubah
6. Al Kaf	Al Kaf
7. Al Qasrayn	Al Qasrayn
8. Qafsah	Qafsah
9. Qabis	Qabis
10. Madaniyin	Madaniyin
11. Sidi Bu Zayd	Sidi Bu Zayd
12. Safaquis	Safaquis
13. Al Mahdiyah	Al Mahdiyah
14. Al Munastir	Al Munastir
15. Susah	Susah
16. Nabul	Nabul
17. Al Qavrawan	Al Qavrawan
18. Silyanah	Silyanah

(1) TURKEY

(2) The Republic of Turkey

(3) Türkiye

(4) Most of Turkey lies in Asia in the Anatolian Peninsula, bordered on the east by the U.S.S.R. and Iran, and on the south by Iraq and Syria. The small European part of Turkey, separated by the Straits of Bosporus, abuts upon Greece and Bulgaria.

(5) Ankara

(6) Turkey comprises 67 administrative units known as provinces or "Ils."

Ils	Capitals
1. Adana	Adana

2.	Adiyaman	Adiyaman
3.	Afyonkarahisar	Afyonkarahisar
4.	Ağri	Karaköse
5.	Amasya	Amasya
6.	Ankara	Ankara
7.	Antalya	Antalya
8.	Artvin	Artvin
9.	Aydin	Aydin
10.	Balikesir	Balikesir
11.	Bilecik	Bilecik
12.	Bingöl	Bingöl
13.	Bitlis	Bitlis
14.	Bolu	Bolu
15.	Burdur	Burdur
16.	Bursa	Bursa
17.	Çanakkale	Çanakkale
18.	Çankiri	Çankiri
19.	Çorum	Çorum
20.	Denizli	Denizli
21.	Diyarbakir	Diyarbakir
22.	Edirne	Edirne
23.	Elâziğ	Elâziğ
24.	Erzincan	Erzincan
25.	Erzurum	Erzurum
26.	Eskişehir	Eskişehir
27.	Gaziantep	Gaziantep
28.	Gireşun	Gireşun
29.	Gümüşane	Gümüşane
30.	Hakkari	Cölemerik
31.	Hatay	Antakya
32.	İsparta	İsparta
33.	İçel	Mersin
34.	İstanbul	İstanbul
35.	İzmir	İzmir
36.	Kars	Kars
37.	Kastamonu	Kastamonu
38.	Kayseri	Kayseri
39.	Kirklareli	Kirklareli
40.	Kirşehir	Kirşehir
41.	Kocaeli	İzmit
42.	Konya	Konya
43.	Kütahya	Kütahya
44.	Malatya	Malatya
45.	Manisa	Manisa
46.	Maraş	Maraş
47.	Mardin	Mardin
48.	Muğla	Muğla
49.	Muş	Muş
50.	Nevşehir	Nevşehir
51.	Niğde	Niğde
52.	Ordu	Ordu

53.	Rize	Rize
54.	Sakarya	Adapazari
55.	Samsun	Samsun
56.	Siirt	Siirt
57.	Sinop	Sinop
58.	Sivas	Sivas
59.	Tekirdağ	Tekirdağ
60.	Tokat	Tokat
61.	Trabzon	Trabzon
62.	Tunceli	Kalan
63.	Urfa	Urfa
64.	Uşak	Uşak
65.	Van	Van
66.	Yozgat	Yozgat
67.	Zonguldak	Zonguldak

(1)   TURKS AND CAICOS ISLANDS

(2)   Turks and Caicos Islands

(3)   Turks and Caicos Islands

(4)   The Turks and Caicos consist of 30 small island cays. They are geographically part of the Bahamas extremity of which they form the southeasterly archipelago.

(5)   Cockburn Town, Grand Turk Island

(6)   Turks and Caicos comprise 6 administrative units known as districts.

Districts	Capitals
1. Grand Turk	Cockburn Town
2. South Caicos	Cockburn Harbor
3. Providenciales	Blue Hills
4. North Caicos	Kew
5. Salt Cay	Salt Cay Town
6. Middle Caicos	Bambarra

(1)   TUVALU

(2)   Tuvalu

(3)   Tuvalu

(4) Tuvalu is a scattered group of nine small atolls, extending 350 miles from north to south, in the western Pacific Ocean. Its nearest neighbors are Fiji to the south, Kiribati to the north, and Solomon Islands to the west.

(5) Vaiaku, Funafuti Island

(6) Tuvalu comprises 8 administrative units known as island councils.

<u>Island Councils</u>
1. Nanumea
2. Nanumanga
3. Niutao
4. Nui
5. Vaitupu
6. Nukufetau
7. Funafuti
8. Nukulaelae

(1) UGANDA

(2) The Republic of Uganda

(3) The Republic of Uganda

(4) Uganda is an equatorial country in East Africa, bordered by Sudan to the north; Zaïre to the west; Kenya to the east; and Rwanda, Tanzania, and Lake Victoria to the south.

(5) Kampala

(6) Uganda comprises 33 administrative units known as districts.

Districts	Capitals
1. Apac	Apac
2. Arua	Arua
3. Bundibugyo	Bundibugyo
4. Bushenyi	Bushenyi
5. Gulu	Gulu
6. Hoima	Hoima
7. Iganga	Iganga
8. Jinja	Jinja
9. Kabale	Kabale
10. Kabarole	Kabarole
11. Kampala	Kampala
12. Kamuli	Kamuli
13. Kapchorwa	Kapchorwa

14.	Kasese	Kasese
15.	Kitgum	Kitgum
16.	Kotido	Kotido
17.	Kumi	Kumi
18.	Lira	Lira
19.	Luwero	Luwero
20.	Musaka	Musaka
21.	Masindi	Masindi
22.	Mbale	Mbale
23.	Mbarara	Mbarara
24.	Moroto	Moroto
25.	Moyo	Moyo
26.	Mpigi	Mpigi
27.	Mubende	Mubende
28.	Mukono	Mukono
29.	Nebbi	Nebbi
30.	Rakai	Rakai
31.	Rukungiri	Rukungiri
32.	Soroti	Soroti
33.	Tororo	Tororo

(1) U.S.S.R.

(2) The Union of Soviet Socialist Republics

(3) Soyuz Sovetskich Socialisticeskich Respublik

(4) The U.S.S.R., the largest country in the world, extends for over 6,000 miles from the Baltic to the Pacific Ocean, and for 3,000 miles from north to south. Its western frontier is bordered by Norway, Finland, Poland, Czechoslovakia, Hungary, and Romania. On its south is Turkey, Iran, Afghanistan, China, Mongolia, and Korea.

(5) Moscow

(6) The U.S.S.R. comprises 173 major administrative units; 15 Soviet Socialist Republics (S.S.R.), 20 Autonomous Soviet Socialist Republics (A.S.S.R.), 10 national territories or "krays," 8 autonomos regions or "autonomous oblasts" and 120 regions or "oblasts."

Soviet Socialist Republics	Capitals
1. Azerbaizhan	Baku
2. Armenian	Yerevan
3. Byelorussian	Minsk
4. Georgian	Tbilisi
5. Estonian	Tallinn

166

6.	Kazakh	Alma-Ata
7.	Kirghiz	Frunze
8.	Latvian	Riga
9.	Lithuanian	Vilnius
10.	Moldavian	Kishinev
11.	Russian (S.F.S.R.)	Moscow
12.	Tadzhik	Dushanbe
13.	Turkmen	Ashkhabad
14.	Ukranian	Kiev
15.	Uzbeck	Tashkent

Autonomous Soviet Socialist Republics		Capitals
16.	Bashkir	Ufa
17.	Buryat	Ulan-Ude
18.	Chechen-Ingush	Grozny
19.	Chuvash	Cheboksary
20.	Daghestan	Makhachkala
21.	Kabardino-Balkar	Nalchik
22.	Kalmyk	Elista
23.	Karelian	Petrozavodsk
24.	Komi	Syktyvkar
25.	Mari	Yoshkar-Ola
26.	Mordovian	Saransk
27.	North Ossetian	Ordzhonikidze
28.	Tatar	Kazan
29.	Tuva	Kyzyl
30.	Udmart	Izhevsk
31.	Yakut	Yakutsk
32.	Nakhichevan	Nakhichevan
33.	Abkhasian	Sukhumi
34.	Adzhar	Batumi
35.	Kara-Kalpak	Nukus

Krays		Capitals
36.	Taymyr	Dudinka
37.	Evenki	Tura
38.	Nenets	Naryan-Mar
39.	Ust-Orda-Buryat	Ust-Ordynsky
40.	Koryak	Palana
41.	Chukchi	Anadyr
42.	Komi-Permyak	Kudymkar
43.	Khanty-Mansiysk	Khanty-Mansiysk
44.	Yamalo-Nenets	Salekhard
45.	Aga-Buryat	Aginskoye

Autonomous Oblasts		Capitals
46.	Adygei	Maikop
47.	Gorno-Altai	Gorno-Altaisk
48.	Jewish	Birobidzhan
49.	Kharacheyewo-Cherkess	Cherkessk

50.	Khakass	Abakan
51.	Nagorno-Karabakh	Stepanokert
52.	South Ossetian	Tskhinvali
53.	Gorno-Badakhshan	Khorog

Oblasts		Capitals
54.	Amur	Blagoveshchensk
55.	Archangel	Archangel
56.	Astrakhan	Astrakhan
57.	Belgorod	Belgorod
58.	Bryansk	Bryansk
59.	Chelyabinsk	Chelyabinsk
60.	Chita	Chita
61.	Gorki	Gorki
62.	Irkutsk	Irkutsk
63.	Ivanovo	Ivanovo
64.	Kaluga	Kaluga
65.	Kalinin	Kalinin
66.	Kaliningrad	Kaliningrad
67.	Kamchatka	Petropavlovsk-Kamchatsky
68.	Kemerovo	Kemerovo
69.	Kirov	Kirov
70.	Kostroma	Kostroma
71.	Kuibyshev	Kuibyshev
72.	Kurgan	Kurgan
73.	Kursk	Kursk
74.	Leningrad	Leningrad
75.	Lipetsk	Lipetsk
76.	Magadan	Magadan
77.	Moscow	Moscow
78.	Murmansk	Murmansk
79.	Novgorod	Novgorod
80.	Novosibirsk	Novosibirsk
81.	Omsk	Omsk
82.	Orel	Orel
83.	Orenburg	Orenburg
84.	Penza	Penza
85.	Perm	Perm
86.	Pskov	Pskov
87.	Rostov	Rostov-On-Don
88.	Ryazan	Ryazan
89.	Sakhalin	Yuzhno-Sakhalinsk
90.	Saratov	Saratov
91.	Smolensk	Smolensk
92.	Sverdlovsk	Sverdlovsk
93.	Tambov	Tambov
94.	Tomsk	Tomsk
95.	Tula	Tula
96.	Tyumen	Tyumen
97.	Ulyanovsk	Ulyanovsk
98.	Vladimir	Vladimir

99.	Volgograd	Volgograd
100.	Vologda	Vologda
101.	Voronezh	Voronezh
102.	Yaroslavl	Yaroslavl
103.	Cherkassy	Cherkassy
104.	Chernigov	Chernigov
105.	Chernovtzy	Chernovtzy
106.	Crimea	Simferopol
107.	Dniepropetrovsk	Dniepropetrovsk
108.	Donetsk	Donetsk
109.	Ivano-Frankovsk	Ivano-Frankovsk
110.	Khmelnitsky	Khmelnitsky
111.	Kharkov	Kharkov
112.	Kherson	Kherson
113.	Kiev	Kiev
114.	Kirovograd	Kirovograd
115.	Lvov	Lvov
116.	Nikolaiev	Nikolaiev
117.	Odessa	Odessa
118.	Poltava	Poltava
119.	Rovno	Rovno
120.	Sumy	Sumy
121.	Ternopol	Ternopol
122.	Vinnitza	Vinnitza
123.	Volhynia	Lutsk
124.	Voroshilovgrad	Voroshilovgrad
125.	Zakarpatskaya	Zakarpatskaya
126.	Zaporozhye	Zaporozhye
127.	Zhitomir	Zhitomir
128.	Brest	Brest
129.	Gomel	Gomel
130.	Grodno	Grodno
131.	Mogilev	Mogilev
132.	Minsk	Minsk
133.	Vitebsk	Vitebsk
134.	Aktyubinsk	Aktyubinsk
135.	Alma-Ata	Alma-Ata
136.	Chimkent	Chimkent
137.	Dzhambul	Dzhambul
138.	Dzhezkazgan	Dzhezkazgan
139.	East Kazakstan	Ust-Kamenogorsk
140.	Guryev	Guryev
141.	Karaganda	Karaganda
142.	Kolchetav	Kolchetav
143.	Kustanai	Kustanai
144.	Kzyl-Orda	Kzyl-Orda
145.	Mangyshlak	Mangyshlak
146.	North Kazakstan	Petropavlovsk
147.	Pavlodar	Pavlodar
148.	Semipalatinsk	Semipalatinsk
149.	Taldy-Kurgan	Taldy-Kurgan

150.	Tselinograd	Tselinograd
151.	Turgai	Turgai
152.	Uralsk	Uralsk
153.	Chardzhou	Chardzhou
154.	Maruy	Maruy
155.	Ashkhabad	Ashkhabad
156.	Tashauz	Tashauz
157.	Krasnovodsk	Krasnovodsk
158.	Andijan	Andijan
159.	Bukhara	Bukhara
160.	Dzhizak	Dzhizak
161.	Ferghana	Ferghana
162.	Kashkadar	Kashkadar
163.	Khorezm	Urgench
164.	Namangan	Namangan
165.	Samarkand	Samarkand
166.	Surkhan-Darya	Termez
167.	Syr-Darya	**Syr-Darya**
168.	Tashkent	Tashkent
169.	Leninabad	Leninabad
170.	Kulyab	Kulyab
171.	Issyk-Kul	Issyk-Kul
172.	Naryn	Naryn
173.	Osh	Osh

(1) UNITED ARAB EMIRATES

(2)   The United Arab Emirates

(3)   Ittihād Al-Imārāt al-^{C}Arabīyah

(4)   U.A.E. extends along the coast of the Arabian Gulf from the base of Qatar to the border with Oman.

(5)   Abu Dhabi

(6)   United Arab Emirates comprises 7 administrative units known as emirates.

Emirates		Capitals
1.	Abu Dhabi	Abu Dhabi
2.	Ajman	Ajman
3.	Dubai	Dubai
4.	Fujairah	Fujairah
5.	Ras al Khaimah	Ras al Khaimah
6.	Sharjah	Sharjah
7.	Umm al Qawain	Umm al Qawain

(2)   United Kingdom

(3)   United Kingdom

(4)   Great Britain is the largest of the islands forming the U.K.
It comprises England, Scotland to the north, and Wales to the
west. It is separated from the coast of western Europe by
the English Channel to the south and by the North Sea to the
east. Ireland lies to the west, across the Irish Sea.

(5)   London

(6)   United Kingdom comprises 92 major administrative units; 1 national capital area, England (Greater London); 6 metropolitan
counties, England; 39 non-metropolitan counties, England;
8 counties, Wales; 9 regions, Scotland; 3 island areas, Scotland; and 26 districts, Northern Ireland.

Metroplitan Counties, England	Capitals
1. Greater Manchester	Manchester
2. Merseyside	Liverpool
3. South Yorkshire	Barnsley
4. Tyne and Wear	Newcastle
5. West Midlands	Birmingham
6. West Yorkshire	Wakefield

Non-Metropolitan Counties, England	Capitals
7. Avon	Bristol
8. Bedfordshire	Bedford
9. Berkshire	Reading
10. Buckinghamshire	Aylesbury
11. Cambridgeshire	Cambridge
12. Cheshire	Chester
13. Cleveland	Middlesborough
14. Cornwall and Isles of Scilly	Truro
15. Cumbria	Carlisle
16. Derbyshire	Matlock
17. Devon	Exeter
18. Dorset	Dorchester
19. Durham	Durham
20. East Sussex	Lewes
21. Essex	Chelmsford
22. Glocestershire	Gloucester
23. Hampshire	Winchester
24. Hereford and Worcester	Worcester
25. Hertfordshire	Hertford
26. Humberside	North Humberside

27.	Isle of Wight	Newport
28.	Kent	Maidstone
29.	Lancashire	Preston
30.	Leicestershire	Leicester
31.	Lincolnshire	Lincoln
32.	Norfolk	Norwich
33.	Northamptonshire	Northampton
34.	Northumberland	Morpeth
35.	North Yorkshire	Northallerton
36.	Nottinghamshire	Nottingham
37.	Oxfordshire	Oxford
38.	Shropshire	Shrewsbury
39.	Somerset	Taunton
40.	Staffordshire	Stafford
41.	Suffolk	Ipswich
42.	Surrey	Kingston-upon-Thames
43.	Warwickshire	Warwick
44.	West Sussex	Chichester
45.	Wiltshire	Trowbridge

Counties, Wales		Capitals
46.	Clwyd	Mold
47.	Dyfed	Carmarthen
48.	Gwent	Cwmbran
49.	Gwynedd	Caernarfon
50.	Mid Glamorgan	Cardiff
51.	South Glamorgan	Cardiff
52.	West Glamorgan	Swansea
53.	Powys	Llandrindod Wells

Regions, Scotland		Capitals
54.	Highland	Inverness
55.	Grampian	Aberdeen
56.	Tayside	Dundee
57.	Fife	Fife
58.	Lothian	Edinburg
59.	Central	Stirling
60.	Borders	Newton St. Boswells
61.	Strathclyde	Glasgow
62.	Dumfries and Galloway	Dumfries

Island Areas, Scotland		Capitals
63.	Orkney	Kirkwall
64.	Shetland	Lerwick
65.	Western Isles	Stornoway, Lewis Island

Districts, Northern Ireland		Capitals
66.	Antrim	Newtownards
67.	Ards	Ards
68.	Armagh	Armagh
69.	Ballymoney	Ballymoney

70.	Banbridge	Banbridge
71.	Belfast	Belfast
72.	Carrickfergus	Carrickfergus
73.	Castlereagh	Castlereagh
74.	Coleraine	Coleraine
75.	Cookstown	Cookstown
76.	Craigavon	Portadown
77.	Down	Downpatrick
78.	Dungannon	Dungannon
79.	Fermanagh	Enniskillen
80.	Larne	Larne
81.	Limavady	Limavady
82.	Lisburn	Lisburn
83.	Londonderry	Londonderry
84.	Magherafelt	Magherafelt
85.	Moyle	Ballycastle
86.	Newry and Mourne	Newry
87.	Newtownabbey	Newtownabbey
88.	North Down	Bangor
89.	Omagh	Omagh
90.	Strabane	Strabane
91.	Ballymena	Ballymena

(1) U.S.A.

(2) The United States of America

(3) The United States of America

(4) The U.S.A. comprises mainly the North American continent between Canada and Mexico. Alaska, to the northwest of Canada, and Hawaii, in the central Pacific Ocean, are two of the 50 states of the U.S.A.

(5) Washington, D.C.

(6) The United States comprises 51 administrative units; 1 federal capital district (Washington, D.C.) and 50 states.

States	Capitals
1. Alabama	Montgomery
2. Alaska	Juneau
3. Arizona	Phoenix
4. Arkansas	Little Rock
5. California	Sacramento
6. Colorado	Denver
7. Connecticut	Hartford
8. Delaware	Dover

9.	Florida	Tallahassee
10.	Georgia	Atlanta
11.	Hawaii	Honolulu
12.	Idaho	Boise
13.	Illinois	Springfield
14.	Indiana	Indianapolis
15.	Iowa	Des Moines
16.	Kansas	Topeka
17.	Kentucky	Frankfort
18.	Louisiana	Baton Rouge
19.	Maine	Augusta
20.	Maryland	Annapolis
21.	Massachusetts	Boston
22.	Michigan	Lansing
23.	Minnesota	St. Paul
24.	Mississippi	Jackson
25.	Missouri	Jefferson City
26.	Montana	Helena
27.	Nebraska	Lincoln
28.	Nevada	Carson City
29.	New Hampshire	Concord
30.	New Jersey	Trenton
31.	New Mexico	Santa Fe
32.	New York	Albany
33.	North Carolina	Raleigh
34.	North Dakota	Bismark
35.	Ohio	Columbus
36.	Oklahoma	Oklahoma City
37.	Oregon	Salem
38.	Pennsylvania	Harrisburg
39.	Rhode Island	Providence
40.	South Carolina	Columbia
41.	South Dakota	Pierre
42.	Tennessee	Nashville
43.	Texas	Austin
44.	Utah	Salt Lake City
45.	Vermont	Montpelier
46.	Virginia	Richmond
47.	Washington	Olympia
48.	West Virginia	Charleston
49.	Wisconsin	Madison
50.	Wyoming	Cheyenne

(1)   U.S. VIRGIN ISLANDS

(2)   United States Virgin Islands

(3)   United States Virgin Islands

(4) The U.S. Virgin Islands consists of three main islands and some 50 smaller islands, situated at the eastern end of the Greater Antilles about 40 miles east of Puerto Rico in the Caribbean.

(5) Charlotte Amalie

(6) U.S. Virgin Islands comprises 2 administrative units known as municipalities.

Municipalities	Capitals
1. St. Croix	Christiansted
2. St. Thomas and St. John	Charlotte Amalie

(1) UPPER VOLTA (Burkina Faso)

(2) The Republic of Upper Volta

(3) République de la Haute-Volta

(4) Upper Volta is a landlocked state in West Africa, surrounded by Mali to the north, Niger to the east, and Benin, Togo, Ghana, and Ivory Coast to the south.

(5) Ouagadougou

(6) Upper Volta comprises 13 administrative units; 5 special municipalities or "communes de plein exercice," and 8 départments. In 1984 the country was renamed Burkina Faso.

Communes de Plein Exercice
1. Goucoy
2. Réo
3. Fada N'Gourma
4. Tenkodogo
5. Kaya

Départments	Capitals
6. Centre	Ouagadougou
7. Volta Noire	Dedougou
8. Hauts Bassins	Bobo-Dioulasso
9. Est	Fada N'Gourma
10. Yatenga	Ouahigouya
11. Centre-Ouest	Koudougou
12. Sahel	Dori
13. Plateaux de Nord-Mossi	Kaya

(1)   URUGUAY

(2)   The Eastern Republic of Uruguay

(3)   Republica Oriental del Uruguay

(4)   Uruguay lies on the southeast coast of South America, with Brazil to the north and Argentina to the west.

(5)   Montevideo

(6)   Uruguay comprises 19 administrative units known as departments.

Departments	Capitals
1. Artigas	Artigas
2. Canelones	Canelones
3. Cerro-Largo	Melo
4. Colonia	Colonia
5. Durazno	Durazno
6. Flores	Trinidad
7. Florida	Florida
8. Lavelleja	Minas
9. Maldonado	Maldonado
10. Montevideo	Montevideo
11. Pay Sandú	Pay Sandú
12. Río Negro	Fray Bentos
13. Rivera	Rivera
14. Rocha	Rocha
15. Salto	Salto
16. San José	San José
17. Soriano	Mercedes
18. Tacuarembó	Tacuarembó
19. Treinta y Tres	Treinta y Tres

(1)   VANUATU

(2)   Republic of Vanuatu

(3)   Ripablik-Blong-Vanuatu

(4)   Vanuatu, formerly the New Hebrides island group, lies about 500 miles west of Fiji, in the Pacific.

(5)   Port-Vila

(6)   Vanuatu comprises 14 administrative units known as constituencies.

<u>Constituencies</u>
1. Banks and Torres
2. Aoba and Maewo
3. Santo, Malo, and Aore
4. Luganville
5. Malakula
6. Ambrym
7. Pentecost
8. Paama
9. Epi
10. Shepherd
11. Efate
12. Port-Vila
13. Tanna
14. Southern Islands

(1) VATICAN CITY STATE

(2) Vatican City State

(3) Stato Della Citta Del Vaticano

(4) In Rome, Vatican City covers an area of 109 acres. Here are found the Palaces of the Lateran and the Vatican. The Papacy claims the Villa of Castelgandolfo.

(5) Vatican City

(6) Vatican City States is governed as a city-state by the Pontifical Committee for the State of the Vatican City. There are no local subdivisions.

(1) VENEZUELA

(2) Republic of Venezuela

(3) República de Venezuela

(4) Venezuela lies on the north coast of South America, bordered by Colombia to the west, Guyana to the east, and Brazil to the south.

(5) Caracas

(6) Venezuela comprises 24 administrative units; 1 federal island

dependency (Margarita Island, capital), 1 federal capital district (Caracas, capital), 2 federal territories, and 20 states.

Federal Territories	Capitals
1. Amazonas	Puerto Ayacucho
2. Delta Amacuro	Tucupita

States	Capitals
3. Anzoátegui	Barcelona
4. Apure	San Fernando
5. Aragua	Marcay
6. Barinas	Barinas
7. Bolívar	Ciudad Bolívar
8. Carabobo	Valencia
9. Cojedes	San Carlos
10. Falcón	Coro
11. Guárico	San Juan
12. Lara	Barquisimeto
13. Mérida	Mérida
14. Miranda	Los Teques
15. Monagas	Maturin
16. Nueva Esparta	La Asunción
17. Portuguesa	Guanare
18. Sucre	Cumaná
19. Táchiro	San Cristóbal
20. Trujillo	Trujillo
21. Yaracuy	San Felipe
22. Zulia	Maracaibo

(1) VIETNAM

(2) The Socialist Republic of Viet-Nam

(3) Viet-Nam Dan-chu Cong-hoa

(4) Vietnam is in Southeast Asia, bordered to the north by China, to the west by Laos and Kampuchea, and to the east by the South China Sea.

(5) Hanoi

(6) Vietnam comprises 39 administrative units; 36 provinces and 3 special municipalities.

Provinces	Capitals
1. Lai Chau	Lai Chau
2. Son La	Son La
3. Hoang Lien Son	Lau Cai

178

4.	Ha Tuyen	Ha Tuyen
5.	Cao Bang	Cao Bang
6.	Lang Son	Lang Son
7.	Bac Thai	Thai Nguyen
8.	Quang Ninh	Hong Gai
9.	Vinh Phu	Viet Tri
10.	Ha Bac	Bac Giang
11.	Ha Son Binh	Hoa Binh
12.	Hai Hung	Hai Duong
13.	Thai Binh	Thai Binh
14.	Ha Nam Ninh	Ninh Binh
15.	Thanh Hoa	Thanh Hoa
16.	Nghe Tinh	Vinh
17.	Binh Tri Thien	Hue
18.	Quang Nam-Da-Nang	Da Nang
19.	Nghia Binh	Qui Nhon
20.	Gia Lai-Kon Tum	Cong Tum
21.	Dac Lac	Buon Me Thuot
22.	Phu Khanh	Nha Trang
23.	Lam Dong	Da Lat
24.	Thuan Hai	Phan Thiet
25.	Dong Nai	Bien Hoa
26.	Song Be	Thu Dau Mot
27.	Tay Ninh	Tay Ninh
28.	Long An	Tan-An
29.	Dong Thap	Cao Lanh
30.	Tien Giang	My-Tho
31.	Ben Tre	Ben Tre
32.	Cuu Long	Vinh Long
33.	An-Giang	Long-Xuyen
34.	Hau Giang	Can Tho
35.	Kien Giang	Rach Gia
36.	Minh Hai	Bac Lieu

Special Municipalities
37. Hanoi
38. Haiphong
39. Ho Chi Minh City

(1) WAKE ISLAND

(2) Wake Island, U.S. External Territory

(3) Wake Island, U.S. External Territory

(4) Wake Island and its neighbors, Wilkes and Peale Islands, are
     in the Pacific, 2064 km. east of Guam, and 3700 km. west of
     Hawaii.

(5) Wake Islet

(6) Wake Island is a U.S. Air Force Base and a N.O.A.A. U.S. National Weather Service Station. There are no local subdivisions.

(1) WALLIS AND FUTUNA

(2) French Overseas Territory of Wallis and Tutuna

(3) Îles Wallis et Futuna Territoire Outremer

(4) Wallis and Futuna are located north of Fiji and west of Samoa. The number of islets in the two groups totals 24.

(5) Mata Utu, Wallis Island

(6) Wallis and Futuna Islands comprise 5 administrative units known as districts.

Districts	Capitals
1. Hanake	Hanake
2. Hihifo	Hihifo
3. Mua	Mua
4. Singave	Singave
5. Alo	Alo

(1) WEST GERMANY

(2) Federal Republic of Germany

(3) Bundesrepublik Deutschland

(4) West Germany is located in Central Europe. It is bounded by the North Sea and Denmark on the north; by East Germany and Czechoslovakia on the east; by Switzerland and Austria on the south; and by France, Luxembourg, Belgium, the Netherlands, and the North Sea on the west.

(5) Bonn

(6) West Germany comprises 11 administrative units; 1 special area (West Berlin), and 10 states or "lander."

Lander	Capitals
1. Schleswig-Holstein	Kiel

2.	Hamburg	Hamburg
3.	Lower Saxony	Hanover
4.	Bremen	Bremen
5.	North Rhine Westphalia	Dusseldorf
6.	Hesse	Wiesbaden
7.	Rhineland Palatinate	Mainz
8.	Baden-Württemberg	Stuttgart
9.	Bavaria	Munich
10.	Saarland	Saarbrücken

(1) WESTERN SAMOA

(2) The Independent State of Western Samoa

(3) Samoa-I-Sisifo

(4) Samoa lies in central Polynesia, 2,400 km. north of New Zealand, and consists of two large and seven small islands. They lie between 13° and 15° south latitude and 171° and 173° west longitude.

(5) Apia

(6) Western Samoa comprises 13 administrative units; 2 island regions and 11 political districts.

Island Regions	Capitals
1. Upolu	Apia
2. Savai'i	Palauli

Political Districts
3.	A'ana
4.	Aiga-i-le-tai
5.	Atua
6.	Tuamasaga
7.	Va'a-o-Fonoti
8.	Fa'asaleleaga
9.	Gaga'emauga
10.	Paulauli
11.	Satupa'itea
12.	Yaisigano
13.	Gagaifomauga

(1)   YUGOSLAVIA

(2)   The Socialist Federal Republic of Yugoslavia

(3)   Federnativan Norodna Republika Jugoslavija

(4)   Yugoslavia is bounded in the north by Austria and Hungary,
      in the northeast by Romania, in the east by Bulgaria, in the
      south by Greece, and in the west by Albania, the Adriatic
      Sea, and Italy.

(5)   Belgrade

(6)   Yugoslavia comprises 8 administrative units; 2 autonomous
      provinces and 6 federal republics.

Autonomous Provinces	Capitals
1. Kosovo	Priština
2. Vojvodina	Novi Sad

Federal Republics	Capitals
3. Crna Gora	Titograd
4. Bosnia and Herzegovina	Saravejo
5. Croatia	Zagreb
6. Macedonia	Skopje
7. Slovenia	Ljubljana
8. Serbia	Belgrade

(1)   ZAÏRE

(2)   The Republic of Zaïre

(3)   République du Zaïre

(4)   Zaïre lies in central Africa, bordered by the Congo to the
      northwest; by the Central African Republic and Sudan to the
      north; by Uganda, Rwanda, Burundi, and Tanzania to the
      east; and by Zambia and Angola to the south.

(5)   Kinshasa

(6)   Zaïre comprises 9 administrative units; 1 federal capital terri-
      tory (Kinshasa), and 8 regions.

Regions	Capitals
1. Bandundu	Bandundu
2. Bas-Zaïre	Matadi

3.	Equateur	Mbandaka
4.	Haute-Zaïre	Kisangani
5.	Kasai Occidental	Kananga
6.	Kasai Oriental	Mbuji-Mayi
7.	Kivu	Bukavu
8.	Shaba	Lumumbashi

(1) ZAMBIA

(2) The Republic of Zambia

(3) The Republic of Zambia

(4) Zambia is a landlocked state in central Africa, bordered to the
      north by Tanzania; to the east by Malawi and Mozambique;
      to the south by Zimbabwe, Botswana, and Namibia; to the
      west by Angola; and to the north by Zaïre.

(5) Lusaka

(6) Zambia comprises 9 administrative units known as provinces.

Provinces		Capitals
1.	Northern	Kasama
2.	Western	Mongu
3.	Southern	Livingstone
4.	Eastern	Chipata
5.	North-Western	Solwezi
6.	Luapula	Mansa
7.	Central	Kabwe
8.	Copperbelt	Ndola
9.	Lusaka	Lusaka

(1) ZIMBABWE

(2) The Republic of Zimbabwe

(3) The Republic of Zimbabwe

(4) Zimbabwe is situated between the northern border of the
      Transvaal and the Zambezi River, and is bordered on the
      east by Mozambique and on the west by Botswana.

(5) Harare

(6) Zimbabwe comprises 7 administrative units known as provinces.

Provinces	Capitals
1. Manicaland	Umtali
2. Midlands	Gwelo
3. Mashonaland North	Sinola
4. Mashonaland South	Harare
5. Victoria	Fort Victoria
6. Matabeleland North	Bulawayo
7. Matabeleland South	Gwanda

Agusan del Norte 127
Agusan del Sur 128
Ahmadi 85
Ahuachapan 46
Ahvenanmaa 50
Ahwaz 71
Aibonito 133
Aichi 81
Aiga-i-le-tai 181
Ailinglapalap 95
Ailuk 95
Aimelik Municipality 11
Ain 51
Aïn-Chock-Hay-Hassani 103
Aïoun el Atrous 97
Airai Municipality 11
Aisén 30
Aisén Del Gen. Carlos Ibáñez
   del Campo 29
Aisne 51
Aitutaki 36
Aiwo 106
Aizawl 69
Ajaccio 50
Ajman 170
Ajoupa Bouillon 97
Akaroa 111
Akerhus 120
Akhaïa 58
Akita 80
Akjoujt 97
Akko 75
Aklan 127
Akonolinga 24
Akposso 158
Akrotiri 39
Aktyubinsk 169
Akure 116
Akureyra 68
Akyab 22
Al Asimah 82
Al-Bahah 141
Al Bahr Al Ahmar 151
Al Baidha 119
Al Balqa 82
Al Biqa 86
Al Buhayrah 151
Al Fâshir 151
Al Ghaydah 148
Al Hadd 9
Al-Hoceima 103

Al Hufuf 141
Al Istiwā-Īyahal Al Gharbīyah
   151
Al Istiwā-Īyahal Ash Sharqīyah
   151
Al Janub 86
Al-Jawf 141
Al Kaf 162
Al Karak 82
Al Khabura 122
Al Khalil 82
Al Khawr 134
Al Khurtūm 151
Al Mahdiyah 162
Al Mahwit 119
Al Masanaa 122
Al Mudaibi 121
Al Mudhayrib 122
Al Munastir 162
Al Qasrayn 162
Al Qavrawan 162
Al Quds 82
Alabama 173
Alagoas 19
Alejuela 36
Alajuelita 37
Alaska 173
Alba 136
Alba Iulia 136
Albany 174
Albay 127
Alberta 25
Albi 52
Albina 152
Ålborg 41
Aldabra 20
Alderney 28
Aleg 97
Alençon 52
Aleppo 155
Alessandria 78
Alexandra (New Zealand) 114
Alexandra (Romania) 136
Alexandria 45
Alexandro 145
Alexandroupolis 58
Aley 86
Alfaro Ruíz 37
Alger 3
Algiers 3
Alhucemas 149

Ali Sahih 41
Alice Town 9
Aljunied 144
Allada 13
Allier 51
Alma-Ata 167
Alo 180
Alofau 4
Alofi 117
Alonso de Ibañez 17
Alor Star 92
Alotau 124
Alpes (Haute-) 51
Alpes-de-Haute-Provence 51
Alpes-Maritîmes 51
Alsace 50
Alta Verapaz 62
Altay 102
Altdorf 154
Altima Esperanza 30
Alto Paraná 125
Alvarado 37
Älvsborg 153
Am-Timan 27
Amaara 72
Amambay 125
Amapá 19
Amasya 163
Amazonas 19
Amazonas (Peru) 126
Amazonas (Venezuela) 178
Amb 123
Ambato 44
Ambon 71
Ambrym 177
Amioun 86
Amlamé 158
Amman 82
Amozas (Colombia) 33
Amparai 150
Amphissa 58
Ampurímac 126
Amsterdam 107
Amur 168
Amuri 110
An-Giang 179
An Nīl 151
An Nīl Al Azraq 151
Anadyr 167
Anambra 116
Añasco 134

Anbaar 72
Ancash 126
Andaman And Nicobar Islands 69
Andhra Pradesh 69
Andijan 170
Andorra-La-Vella 4
Andreas 74
Andrés/Bañez 17
Andros and the Berry Islands 9
Andros/Fresh Creek 9
Andros/Kemps Bay 9
Anécho 158
Anegada 20
Anetan 106
Ang Mo Kio 145
Angél Sandoval 18
Angeles 128
Angers 52
Angmagssalik 59
Angol 30
Angoulême 51
Angra do Heroismo 131
Angthong 157
Anguar Municipality 11
Anhui 31
Anibar 106
Anibare 106
Ankara 162
Anna 106
Annaba 3
Annapolis 174
Annecy 52
Anse-Bertrand 60
Anse la Raye 139
Anses d'Arlets 97
Anson 145
Ansongo 94
Antakya 163
Antalya 163
Antananarivo 90
Antártica Chilena 30
Antioquia 34
Antique 127
Antique Guatemala 62
Antofagasta 29
Antrim 172
Antwerpen 12
Anuradhapura 150
Anzoátegui 178

Aoba and Maewo 177
Aomori 80
Aosta 76
Apac 165
Apia 181
Aplahoué 14
Appenzell 154
Apure 178
Aquaviva 140
Aquila 77
Aquitaine 50
Aracajú 19
Arad 136
Aragua 178
Arakan 22
Arani 16
Aranuki 84
Arauca 34
Arauco 30
Arawa 124
Arba Minch 47
Arbeel 72
Arbory 74
Arcadia 58
Arce 17
Archangel 168
Archipiélago de Colon 45
Ardèche 51
Ardennes 51
Ards 172
Arecibo 133
Arequipa 126
Arezzo 76
Arges 136
Argostolion 58
Argolis 58
Arhangay 101
Ari 93
Arica 29
Ariège 51
Arima 161
Arizona 173
Arkansas 173
Arkanes 68
Arlon 12
Armagh 172
Armenia 34
Armenian S.S.R. 166
Arnessýsla 68
Arnhem 107
Arno 95

Arondal 121
Arorae 84
Arque 16
Arras 52
Arrowtown 114
Arroyo 133
Arta 58
Artibonite 65
Artigas 176
Artvin 163
Arua 165
Aruba 108
Arunachal Pradesh 69
Arusha 156
Arussi 47
Arvayheer 102
As Salt 82
Asan 61
Ascensin 137
Ascoli Piceno 78
Aserri 36
Ash Shamal 86
Ash Shamālīyah 151
Ashanti 56
Ashburton Borough (New Zealand) 113
Ashburton County (New Zealand) 111
Ashkhabad 170
Ashley 111
Ashqelon 75
Asir 141
Asmara 47
Assaba 97
Assam 69
Assela 47
Assen 107
Asti 78
Astrakhan 168
Asunción 125
Asu 4
Aswân 45
Asyût 45
Atacama 29
Atafu 159
Atahuallpa 17
Atakora 13
Atakpamé 158
Atar 97
Atenas 37
Athens 57

Athiémé 13
Ati 27
Atiu 36
Atlanta 174
Atlántico 34
Atlantida 66
Atlantique 13
Attica 57
Attopeu 86
Atua 181
Aube 51
Auch 51
Auckland 111
Aude 51
Augusta 174
Auki 146
Aur 95
Aurillac 51
Aurora 128
Ausser-Rhoden 154
Aust-Agder 121
Austin 174
Australian Capital Territory 8
Austur-Bardhastrandarsýsla 68
Austur-Húnavatnssýsla 68
Austur-Skaftafellssýsla 68
Auvergne 50
Auxerre 52
Avaroa 17
Avarua 35
Avatela 117
Avau 4
Aveiro 132
Avellino 77
Aveyron 51
Avignon 52
Aviléz 17
Avon 171
Avrankou 13
Awabi 121
Awassa 47
Ayacucho 126
Aydin 163
Ayer Rajah 145
Aylesbury 171
Ayopaya 16
Azerbaizhan S.S.R. 166
Azilal 103
Azogues 44
Azua 42

Azua de Compostella 42
Azuay 44
Azurduy 16

Ba 49
Baabda 86
Baalbek 86
Babahoyo 44
Babylon 72
Bac Giang 179
Bac Lieu 179
Bac Thai 179
Bacău 136
Bacolod 127
Bacolod Chartered City 129
Bács-Kiskun 67
Badakhsan 1
Baden-Württemberg 181
Badghis 1
Badu Island 160
Badulla 150
Baerhum 120
Bafang 24
Bafatá 64
Bafia 24
Bafilo 159
Bafoulabe 94
Bafoussam 23
Bagaces 37
Baghdad 72
Baghlan 1
Baglung 107
Bagmati 106
Bago 129
Baguio 128
Bahia 19
Bahla 121
Bahoruco 42
Bahr Al Ghazal 151
Baia Mare 136
Baidoa 146
Baie-Mahault 60
Baillif 60
Bairiki 84
Bais 129
Baiti 106
Baja California Norte 99
Baja California Sur 99
Baja Verapaz 62
Bajah 162
Bajaur 123

191

Bid Bid 122
Biddiya 122
Bié 5
Bielskie 130
Bielsko Biala 130
Bien Hoa 179
Bignona 142
Bihar 69
Bihor 136
Bilad Bani Bu Hassan 122
Bilecik 163
Biliran 128
Bilma 115
Bilostockie 130
Biltine 27
Bimini 9
Binh Tri Thien 179
Bíobío 29
Bioko 47
Biombo 64
Birao 27
Biratnager 106
Bird 143
Birkat al Mawz 121
Birkenhead 111
Birmingham (U.K.) 171
Birni N'Gaoure 116
Birni N'Konni 115
Birobidzhan 167
Bishah 141
Biskra 3
Bismark 174
Bissau 64
Bistriţa 136
Bistriţa-Nasaud 136
Bitam 55
Bitlis 163
Bjørnøya 152
Black River (Jamaica) 79
Black River (Mauritius) 98
Blagoevgrad 21
Blagoveshchensk 168
Blantyre 91
Blekinge 153
Blenheim 113
Blida 3
Bloemfontein 147
Blois 51
Blönduós 68
Blowing Point Village 6
Blue Hill 137

Blue Hills 164
Bluefields 115
Bluff 114
Bo 143
Boa Alta 132
Boa Baja 132
Boa Vista 19
Boac 127
Boaco 114
Bobigny 52
Bobo-Dioulasso 175
Bocas del Toro 124
Bodden Town 26
Bodø 121
Boe 106
Boeotia 57
Boffa 63
Bogatá 33
Bogra 10
Bohicon 14
Bohol 127
Boigu Island 160
Boise 174
Bok Kou 83
Boké 63
Bol 27
Bolama-Bijagos 64
Bolands 6
Bolgatanga 56
Bolívar 34
Bolívar (Ecuador) 44
Bolívar (Venezuela) 178
Bologna 76
Bolu 163
Bombay 69
Bonair 108
Bondoukou 79
Bong 88
Bongöl 163
Bongor 27
Bonn 180
Bontoc 126
Boon Lay 145
Boon Teck 145
Booué 55
Bopa 14
Bophuthatswana 147
Boquerón 125
Bor 151
Bordeaux 50
Borders 172

Borgarfjardharsýsla 68
Borgarnes 68
Borgo 140
Borgou 13
Borikane 86
Borkou-Ennedi-Tibesti 27
Bornholms 41
Borno 117
Borongan 127
Borsod-Abaúj-Zemplén 67
Bosnia and Herzegovina 182
Boston 174
Botoşani 136
Bouaflé 79
Bouaké 79
Bouar 27
Bouar-Baboua 27
Bouches-du-Rhône 51
Boueni 98
Bouenza 35
Bougouni 94
Bouillante 60
Bouira 3
Boujdour 103
Boukoumbé 14
Boulemane 103
Boulouparis 108
Boumba-Ngoko 24
Bouna 79
Boundiali 79
Bourail 108
Bourem 94
Bourg-en-Bresse 51
Bourges 51
Bourgogne 50
Boyacá 34
Boyerahmadi Va Kohkiluyeh 71
Bozoum 27
Brabant 12
Braciosa Bay 146
Braddan 74
Braddell Heights 144
Braga 132
Bragança 132
Braila 136
Brakna 97
Bras-Panon 135
Brasilia 19
Braşov 136
Bratislava 40
Brava 25

Brazzaville 35
Bregenz 8
Bremen 181
Brescia 77
Brest 169
Bretagne 50
Bria 27
Brickwords 144
Bride 74
Bridgetown 11
Brikama 56
Brindisi 77
Brisbane 8
Bristol 171
British Columbia 25
Brno 40
Brokopondo 152
Brong-Ahafo 56
Bruce 111
Bruges 12
Brunei/Muara 21
Brussels 12
Bryansk 168
Bu'aale 146
Buada 106
Buala 146
Buba 64
Bubanza 23
Bucaramanga 34
Buchanan 88
Bucharest 135
Buckinghamshire 171
Budapest 67
Búdardalur 68
Buea 23
Buenos Aires (Argentina) 7
Buenos Aires (Costa Rica) 38
Bugti 123
Bujumbura 23
Bukavu 183
Bukh 122
Bukhara 170
Bukidnon 127
Bukit Batok 145
Bukit Ho Swee 145
Bukit Merah 144
Bukit Panjang 144
Bukit Timah 144
Bukoba 156
Bulacan 127
Bulawayo 184

Cap-Haitien 65
Cap-Vert 142
Cape Coast 56
Cape (South Africa) 147
Cape Town 147
Capellen 89
Capesterre-de-Guadeloupe 60
Capesterre-de-Marie-Galante
60
Capinota 17
Capisterre (St. John, St.
Kitts) 138
Capisterre (St. Paul, St.
Kitts) 138
Capitán Prat 30
Capiz 127
Caqueta 34
Caprivi East 105
Caprivi West 105
Carabobo 178
Caracas 177
Carangas 17
Caraş-Severin 136
Carbet 97
Carcassonne 51
Carchi 44
Cardiff 172
Carlisle (Antigua) 6
Carlisle (U.K.) 171
Carlow 73
Carmarthen 172
Carmona 5
Carolina 132
Caroni 161
Carrasco 17
Carrick-On-Shannon 73
Carrickfergus 173
Carrillo 38
Carson City 174
Cartagena 34
Cartago 36
Carterton 113
Casablanca-Anfa 103
Casanare 34
Cascade 118
Case-Pilote 97
Caserta 77
Cassamance 142
Castel 28
Castellón 149
Castelo Branco 132

Castlebar 73
Castlereagh 173
Castries 138
Castro 30
Cat Island 9
Catamarca 7
Catanduanes 127
Catania 78
Cataño 133
Catanzaro 76
Catarman 127
Catbalogan 127
Catió 64
Cauca 34
Cautín 30
Cavan 73
Cavite 127
Caxito 5
Cayenne 53
Cayey 133
Cayman Brac 26
Cayon 138
Ceará 19
Cebu 127
Cebu Chartered City 129
Cedarhurst 15
Ceerigaabo 146
Ceiba 133
Central (Alajuela) 37
Central And Western (Hong
Kong) 66
Central (Bahrain) 9
Central (Cartago) 37
Central (Fiji) 49
Central (Gambia) 56
Central (Ghana) 56
Central (Heredia) 37
Central (Israel) 75
Central Islands (Solomons) 146
Central (Kenya) 84
Central (Limon) 38
Central Luzon 128
Central (Malawi) 91
Central Mindanao 128
Central (Montserrat) 102
Central (Papua New Guinea)
124
Central (Paraguay) 125
Central (Puntarenas) 38
Central (San Jose) 36
Central (Scotland) 172

Central (Sudan) 151
Central (Torres Straight) 160
Central Visayas 128
Central (Zambia) 183
Centrale (Togo)
Centre de Flacq 98
Centre (France) 50
Centre (Haiti) 65
Centre-Ouest (Upper Volta)
   175
Centre-Sud (Cameroon) 23
Centre (Upper Volta) 175
Cercado (Bení) 18
Cercado (Cochabamba) 16
Cercado (Oruro) 17
Cercado (Tarija) 17
Cerro de Pasco 126
Cerro-Largo 176
César 34
České Budějovice 40
Ceuta 149
Chachapoyas 126
Cha-choengsao 157
Chaco 7
Chafarinas 149
Chaguanos 161
Chai-nat 157
Chala Kanoa (T.T.P.I.) 161
Chalatenango 46
Chalcis 57
Chalon Kanao Town 120
Châlons-sur-Marne 52
Chambéry 52
Champagne-Ardenne 50
Chañaral 30
Chandigarh 69
Changchun 31
Changhua 32
Changi 144
Changsha 31
Chanthaburi 157
Chaouen 103
Chapare 17
Chardzhou 170
Charente 51
Charente-Maritime 51
Charcas 17
Chari-Banguirmi 27
Charikar 1
Charleston 174
Charlestown (Nevis) 138

Charleville-Mézières 51
Charlotte Amalie 175
Charlotte (St. Vincent) 140
Charlottetown 25
Chartres 51
Châteaubelair 139
Châteauroux 51
Chatham Islands 111
Chaumont 52
Chauncey 140
Chayanta 17
Chayaphum 157
Cheboksary 167
Chechen-Ingush 167
Cheju 148
Chekha 15
Chelm 130
Chelmsford 171
Chelmskie 130
Chelyabinsk 168
Chemin Grenier 98
Cheng San 144
Ghengdu 31
Cher 51
Cherkassy 169
Cherkessk 167
Chernigov 169
Chernovtzy 169
Cheshire 171
Chester 171
Chetumal 100
Cheviot 110
Cheyenne 174
Chiapas 99
Chiayi 32
Chiba 80
Chichester 172
Chiclayo 126
Chiconi 98
Chiengmai 157
Chiengrai 157
Chiesanuova 140
Chieti 77
Chihuahua 99
Chikwawa 91
Chilas 122
Chile Chico 30
Chillán 30
Chiloe 30
Chilpanchingo de los Bravos
   99

Colon (Honduras) 66
Colón (Panama) 124
Colonel Hill 9
Colonia (T.T.P.I.) 161
Colonia (Uruguay) 176
Colorado 173
Columbia 174
Columbus 174
Comayagua 66
Comerioq 133
Comilla 10
Commewijne 152
Como 77
Conakry 63
Concepción (Chile) 29
Concepción (Paraguay) 125
Concord 174
Cong Tum 179
Connecticut 173
Constanta 136
Constantine 3
Cook 110
Cookstown 173
Copán 66
Copenhagen 40
Copiapó 29
Copperbelt 183
Coquimbo 29
Corazo 114
Cordillera 17
Cordillera (Paraguay) 125
Córdoba (Argentina) 7
Córdoba (Colombia) 34
Córdoba (Spain) 149
Cork 73
Cornelio Saavedra 17
Cornwall and Isles of Scilly
171
Coro 178
Coronado 37
Coronel Oveido 125
Coronie 152
Corovodë 2
Corozal (Belize) 13
Corozal (Puerto Rico) 132
Corrèze 51
Corrientes 7
Corse 50
Corse-du-Sud 51
Corse (Haute-) 51
Cortés 66

Çorum 163
Cosenza 77
Cotabato 129
Côte-d'Or 51
Côtes-du-Nord 51
Coto Brus 38
Cotonou 13
Cotopaxi 44
Cottbus 43
Cotton Ground 138
Cotui 43
Cousin 143
Cousine 143
Covasna 136
Craigavon 173
Craiova 136
Creer 26
Cremona 77
Créteil 52
Creuse 51
Creux 28
Crimea 169
Croatia 182
Cromwell 114
Crooked Island 9
Cross River 116
Crna Gora 182
Csongrád 67
Cuando-Cubango 5
Cuanza Norte 5
Cuanza Sul 5
Cúcuta 34
Cuenca 44
Cuenca (Spain) 149
Cuernavaca 99
Cuiabá 19
Cuilapa 62
Culiacán 100
Cumaná 178
Cumbria 171
Cundinamarca 34
Cunene 5
Cuneo 78
Curaçao 108
Curepipe 98
Curicó 30
Curieuse 143
Curridabat 37
Curtiba 19
Cuscatlán 46
Cuu Long 179

Cuvette 35
Cuzco 126
Cwmbran 172
Cyangugu 137
Cyclades 58
Cyrenaica 88
Czech Socialist Republic 40
Czestochawa 130
Czestochowskie 130

Da Lat 179
Da Nang 179
Dabakala 79
Dabola 63
Dac Lac 179
Dacca 10
Dadra and Nagar Haveli 69
Daet 127
Dagana 142
Daghestan 167
Dagupa 128
Dajabón 42
Dakar 142
Dakhlet-Nouadhibou 97
Dakouro 116
Dalaba 63
Dalandzadgad 102
Dalasýsla 68
Dalbandin 123
Daloa 79
Damanhûr 45
Damaraland 105
Damascus 155
Damietta 45
Danané 79
Danao 129
Dandeldhura 107
Dangbo 13
Dangriga 13
Daniel Campos 17
Dank 121
Dannevirke (county) 110
Dannevirke 112
Dapango 158
Dapaon 158
Dapitan 129
Daqahlîya 45
Dar es Salaam 155
Dārfūr 151
Dārfūr Al Janūbīyah 151
Dārfūr Ash Shamālīyah 151

Dargaville 111
Darhan 101
Darién 124
Darnley Island 160
Darrit Uliga Dalap 95
Daru 124
Darwin 8
Dassa-Zoumé 14
Dauan Island 160
Daulat Yar 1
Davao 129
Davao del Norte 128
Davao del Sur 128
Davao Oriental 128
David 124
De La Araucanía 29
De la Kara 158
De Los Lagos 29
Debre Markos 47
Debrecen 67
Dededo 61
Dedougou 175
Dedza 91
Deir-ez-Zor 155
Del Libertador Gen. Bernardo
    O'Higgins 29
Del Maule 29
Delaware 173
Delemont 154
Delhi 69
Delta Amacuro 178
Delta (Singapore) 145
Dembeni 99
Denigomodu 106
Denizli 163
Dennery 139
Denpasar 70
Denver 173
Dera Ismail Khan 123
Dera ͨa 155
Derbyshire 171
Derecen 67
Derna 88
Des Moines 174
Des Plateaux 158
Des Savanes 158
Desamparados 36
Deshaies 60
Desroches 20
Dessie 47
Deva 136

199

Devon 171
Devonport 111
Devonshire (Bermuda) 14
Dewagiri 15
Dhamar 119
Dhangarhi 107
Dhaulagiri 107
Dhekalia 39
Dhofar 121
Diamant 97
Diamaré 24
Diamir 122
Dibbah 122
Dibrë 2
Diego Garcia 20
Diégo-Suarez 90
Diekirch 89
Diffa 115
Digne 51
Digos 128
Dijon 50
Dikhan 134
Dikhil 41
Dili 71
Dimbokro 79
Dîmboviţa 136
Dinajpur 10
Dinguiraye 63
Dioila 94
Diourbel 142
Dipolog 127
Dipolog Chartered City 129
Dir 123
Dire 94
Direction Island 33
Dispur 69
District of Columbia 173
Divo 79
Diwaaniya 72
Diyaala 72
Diyarbakir 163
Dja-et-Lobo 23
Djambala 35
Djelfa 3
Djenne 94
Djougou 14
Dniepropetrovsk 169
Doba 27
Dodecanese 58
Dodoma 156
Dogbo 14

Dogondoutchi 115
Doha 134
Dolisie 35
Dolj 136
Domagnano 140
Domaneab 106
Donegal 73
Donetsk 169
Dong Nai 179
Dong Thap 179
Dorado 133
Dorchester 171
Dordogne 51
Dori 175
Dornod 101
Dornogov́ 101
Dorset 171
Dossa 105
Dosso 115
Dota 37
Douala 23
Doubs 51
Douentza 94
Douglas 74
Dover 173
Dowa 91
Down 173
Downpatrick 173
Drama 58
Drammen 121
Drenthe 107
Dresden 43
Drobeta-Turnu-Severin 136
Drôme 51
Dschang 24
Du Vent 135
Duarte 42
Dubai 170
Dublin 73
Dubréka 63
Ducos 96
Dudinka 167
Duhook 72
Dumaguete 127
Dumbea 108
Dumfries 172
Dumfires and Galloway 172
Dun Laoghaire 73
Duncan Town 9
Duncan Town 9
Dundalk 73
Dundee 172

Dundgov́ 101
Dunedin 113
Dungannon 173
Dunmore Town 9
Dunquiah 151
Durango 99
Durazno 176
Durham (U.K.) 171
Durrës 2
Dusa Marreb 146
Dushanbe 167
Dusseldorf 181
Dyfed 172
Dzaoudzi 99
Dzavhan 102
Dzhambul 169
Dzhezkazgan 169
Dzhizak 170
Dzuun Mod 102

East Azerbaijan 71
East Berbice 64
East Berlin 43
East Coast Bays 111
East Demerara 64
East End 26
East Falkland 48
East Greenland 59
East Kazakstan 169
East New Britain 124
East Sepik 124
East Sussex 171
Eastbourne 113
Eastern (Fiji) 49
Eastern (Ghana) 56
Eastern Highlands 124
Eastern (Hong Kong) 67
Eastern Islands (Temotu) 146
Eastern (Kenya) 84
Eastern (Montserrat) 102
Eastern Samar 127
Eastern (Saudi Arabia) 141
Eastern (Sierra Leone) 143
Eastern (Sudan) 151
Eastern (Torres Straight) 160
Eastern Tutuila 4
Eastern Visayas 128
Eastern (Zambia) 183
Ebeye 95
Ebolowe 24
Ebon 95

Echternach 90
Edea 24
Edessa 58
Edinburg 172
Edirne 163
Edmont 110
Edmonton 25
Efate 177
Egedesminde 59
Eger 67
Ehima 81
Eidi 48
Eisenstadt 8
Eketahuna 110
El Asnam 3
El Cayo 13
El Guarco 37
El Jadida 103
El Kellâa Sraghna 103
El Ladhiqiya 155
El Loa 30
El Oro 44
El Paráiso 66
El Porvenir 123
El Progreso 62
El Quneitra 155
El Rashid 155
El Seibo 43
Elâziǧ 163
Elbasan 2
Elblag 130
Elblaskie 130
Eleuthera/North 9
Eleuthera/South 9
Elia 58
Elías Piña 42
Elista 167
Ellerslie 112
Ellesmere 111
Elqui 30
Eltham 110
Emilia-Romagna 76
Emmore 64
Encamp 4
Encarnación 125
Enga 124
Enna 78
Ennis 73
Enniskillen 173
Enterprise 64
Entre-Deux 135

Filingue 115
Finistère 51
Finnmark 121
Fiord 111
Firenze 76
Fitiuta 4
Flacq 98
Florence 76
Florencia 34
Flores (Costa Rica) 37
Flores (Guatemala) 62
Flores (Uruguay) 176
Florida (U.S.A.) 174
Florida (Bolivia) 17
Florina 58
Flurianópolis 19
Flying Fish Cove 32
Focşani 136
Foggia 77
Fogo 25
Foix 51
Fomboni 35
Fonds Saint-Denis 97
Fontvieille 101
Fonuakula 117
Forécariah 63
Forest 28
Forli 77
Formosa 7
Fort Archambault 27
Fort-de-France 96
Fort-Foureau 24
Fort Liberté 65
Fort-Rousset 35
Fort-Sibut 27
Fort Victoria 184
Fort Wellington 64
Fortaleza 19
Fougamou 55
Foumban 24
Foundiougne 142
Foxton 113
Franceville 54
Franche-Comté 50
Francisco Morazán 65
Francistown 18
François 96
Frankfort 174
Frankfurt an der Oder 43
Franklin 109
Fransfontein 105

Franz Tamayo 16
Fredericton 25
Frederiksborg 41
Frederikshåb 59
Freetown (Sierra Leone) 143
Freeport 9
Fresh Creek 9
Fria 63
Frías 17
Fribourg 154
Friesland 107
Frigate 143
Friuli-Venezia-Giulia 76
Frosinone 77
Frunze 167
Fuerte Olímpo 125
Fujairah 170
Fujian 31
Fukui 80
Fukuoka 81
Fukushima 80
Funafuti 165
Funchal 132
Fuzhou 31
Fyns 41

Gaborone 18
Gabrovo 21
Gabú 64
Gabú Sara 64
Gaga'emauga 181
Gagaifomauga 181
Gagnoa 79
Galaţi 136
Galcaio 146
Galguduud 146
Galle 150
Galway 73
Gam 105
Gamprin 89
Gandaki 106
Gandhinager 69
Gangtok 70
Gansu 31
Gao 93
Gaoual 63
Gap 51
Garbahaarrey 146
Garbîya 45
Gard 51
Gardez 1

Gov́-altay 102
Governor's Harbour 9
Goyave 61
Gozo and Comino 95
Geraldine 113
Graciás 66
Gracias a Dios 66
Gral. Ballivian 18
Gral. Bilboa 17
Gral. F. Román 17
Grampian 172
Gramsh 2
Gran Chaco 17
Granaway 15
Grand Anse 65
Grand Bahama 9
Grand Bassa 88
Grand-Bourg 61
Grand Cape Mount 88
Grand Cayman 26
Grand Jide 88
Grand-Popo 13
Grand-Port 98
Grand-Rivière 97
Grand Rivière Noire 98
Grand-Santi 53
Grand Turk 164
Granma 38
Graubunden 154
Gravenmacher 89
Graz 8
Great Barrier Islands 109
Great Harbour Bay 20
Greater Accra 56
Greater London 171
Greater Manchester 171
Grecia 37
Green Island 113
Green Turtle Cay 9
Greenville 88
Grenada (Nicaragua) 115
Grenada (Spain) 149
Grenadines 139
Grenoble 51
Grenville 60
Grevena 58
Grey 110
Greymouth 113
Greytown 113
Grodno 169
Groningen (Netherlands) 107

Groningen (Surinam) 152
Grootfontein 105
Gros Islet 139
Gros Morne 96
Grosseto 76
Grouville 29
Grozny 167
Guadalajara (Mexico) 99
Guadalajara (Spain) 149
Guadalcanal 146
Guainía 34
Guairá 125
Guajira 34
Gualberto Villarroel 16
Gualo-Roi-Garapan 120
Guanacaste 36
Guanajuato 99
Guanare 178
Guangdong 31
Guangxi Zhuang 31
Guanica 133
Guantánamo 38
Guaranda 44
Guarda 132
Guárico 178
Guatemala City 62
Guatuso 37
Guayama 133
Guayanilla 133
Guayaquil 44
Guayas 44
Guéckédou 63
Guelma 3
Guelmim 104
Guéra 27
Guéret 51
Guernsey 28
Guerrero 99
Guidimaka 97
Guiglo 79
Guimaras 128
Guinée-Forestière 63
Guinée-Maritîme 63
Guinpúzcoa 149
Guira de Melena 38
Guiyang 31
Guizhou 31
Gujarat 69
Gulf 124
Gullbringu 68
Gullbringusýsla 68

Gulu 165
Gumma 80
Gümüşane 163
Gurabo 132
Guryev 169
Gwanda 184
Gwelo 184
Gwent 172
Gwynedd 172
Györ 67
Györ-Sopron 67

Ha 15
Ha Bac 179
Ha Nam Ninh 179
Ha Son Binh 179
Ha Tuyen 179
Ha'apai 159
Haddummati 93
Hadera 75
Hadramaht 148
Haeju 119
Hafnarfjördhur 68
Hai Duong 179
Hai Hong 179
Haifa 75
Ha'il 141
Hainaut 12
Haiphong 179
Hajdú-Bihar 67
Hajjah 119
Haka 22
Hakapehi 54
Hakkari 163
Hakupu 117
Halba 86
Half Tree Hollow 137
Halifax 25
Halland 153
Halle an der Saale 43
Halmstad 153
Hama 155
Hamadan 71
Hamar 121
Hambantota 150
Hamburg 181
Häme 50
Hämeenlinna 50
Hamgyong-namdo 119
Hamgyong-pukto 119
Hamheung (municipality) 118

Hamheung 119
Hamilton (Bermuda) 14
Hamilton (New Zealand) 112
Hammond Island 160
Hampshire 171
Hanake 180
Hanga Roa 44
Hangaroa (Chile) 30
Hanoi 178
Hanover (Jamaica) 79
Hanover (West Germany) 181
Hangzhou 31
Harar 47
Harare 183
Harbin 31
Harbour Island 9
Hargeysa 146
Harghita 136
Harnosand 154
Harper 88
Harrage 47
Harrisburg 174
Hartford 173
Haryana 69
Hasbaïya 86
Haseke 155
Hasselt 12
Hastings 112
Hatay 163
Hatillo 133
Hau Giang 179
Hauraki Plains 109
Haut-Nkam 24
Haute-de-Seine 51
Haute-Guinée 63
Haute-Kotto 27
Haute-Normandie 50
Haute-Nyong 24
Haute-Ogooué 54
Haute-Sanga 23
Haute-Sangha 27
Haute-Zaïre 183
Hauts Bassins 175
Havana 38
Havelock North 112
Havelock (Singapore) 145
Hawaii 174
Hawalli 85
Hawera 110
Hawke's Bay 110
Hay-Mohamed-Aïn Sebaa 103

Kangalsiaq 59
Kangar 92
Kanggye 119
Kango 55
Kangwon 148
Kangwon-do 119
Kani-Keli 99
Kankan 63
Kano 117
Kansas 174
Kanye 18
Kaoh Kong 83
Kaohsiung 32
Kaokoland 105
Kaolack 142
Kapchorwa 165
Kapiti 113
Kaposvár 67
Kara-Kalpak 167
Karachi 123
Karaganda 169
Karaköse 163
Karasburg 105
Karbalaa 72
Karditsa 58
Karelian 167
Karen 22
Karibib 105
Karkuk 72
Karl-Marx-Stadt 43
Karlskrona 153
Karnali 107
Karnataka 69
Kärnten 8
Karonga 91
Karpenissi 57
Kars 163
Karyi 57
Kasai Occidental 183
Kasai Oriental 183
Kasama 183
Kasese 166
Kashkadar 170
Kaskazini 156
Kassalä 151
Kastamonu 163
Kastoria 58
Kasungu 91
Kasupe 91
Katerini 58
Kathmandu 106

Katima Mulilo 105
Katiola 79
Katong 144
Katowickie 130
Kavala 58
Kavango 105
Kavaratti 69
Kavieng 124
Kaw 53
Kawerau 112
Kaya 175
Kayah 22
Kayangel Municipality 12
Kayes 93
Kayseri 163
Kazakh S.S.R. 167
Kazan 167
Keb 83
Kébémer 142
Kecskemét 67
Kedah 92
Kédougou 142
Keelung 32
Keetmanshoop 105
Kefa 47
Kefallenia 58
Keflavík 68
Kegalla 150
Keita 116
Kelantan 92
Kemerovo 168
Kémo-Gribingui 27
Kemps Bay 9
Kendari 70
Kenema 143
Kenieba 94
Kénitra 103
Kent 172
Kentucky 174
Kerala 69
Kerema 124
Kerewan 56
Kerkyra 58
Kerman 71
Kermanshah (province) 71
Kermanshah 71
Kérou 14
Kerry 73
Keski-Suomen 50
Kétou 13
Kew 164

214

Lingayen 127
Lingshi 15
Linguère 142
Linkoping 153
Linz 8
Lipa 128
Lipetsk 168
Lira 166
Lisboa 132
Lisbon 131
Lisburn 173
Lithuanian S.S.R. 167
Litoral 17
Little Cayman 26
Little Rock 173
Littoral (Cameroon) 23
Liverpool 171
Livingstone 183
Livorno 76
Liwa 122
Ljubljana 182
Llandrindod Wells 172
Llanquihue 30
Loayza 16
Lobatse 18
Lobaye 27
Lodź 131
Łódzkie 131
Loei 157
Lofa 88
Loga 116
Logar 1
Logone Occidental 27
Logone Oriental 27
Logone-et-Chari 24
Loikaw 22
Loir 51
Loir-et-Cher 51
Loir (Haute-) 51
Loire-Atlantique 51
Loiret 51
Loiza 132
Loja 44
Lokia 49
Lokossa 13
Lomaniti 49
Lombardia 76
Lom-et-Djerem 24
Lomé 158
Lomza 131
Lomzyński 131

Lonan 74
London (U.K.) 171
Londonerry 173
Long An 179
Long Bay Village 6
Long Island 9
Long-Xuyen 179
Longford 73
Longroño 149
Longwood 137
Longyearbyen 152
Lons-le-Saunier 51
Lopburi 157
Loralai 123
Lorengau 124
Lorestan 71
Loreta 126
Loro Sae 71
Lorrain 96
Lorraine 50
Los Andes 30
Los Angeles (Chile) 30
Los Antas 124
Los Chiles 37
Los Ríos 44
Los Teques 178
Lot 51
Lot-et-Garonne 51
Lothian 172
Louga 142
Louieville 147
Louisiana 174
Lovech 21
Lower Hutt 113
Lower Jamestown 137
Lower Saxony 181
Lozère 52
Luanda 5
Luang Prabang 85
Luapula 183
Lubelskie 131
Lublin 131
Lubombo 153
Lucca 76
Lucea 79
Lucena 127
Lucknow 70
Lüderitz 105
Luganville 177
Lugo 149
Luis Calvo 16

Lukapa 5
Lulea 154
Luma 4
Lumbini 107
Lumphat 83
Lumumbashi 183
Lunda-Norte 5
Lunda-Sul 5
Luquillo 133
Lusaka 183
Lushnjë 2
Luso 5
Lutsk 169
Luwero 166
Luxembourg (Belgium) 12
Luxembourg City 89
Luzern 154
Lvov 169
Lyon 50
Lyttelton 113

Ma'an 82
Maasin 127
Maastricht 107
Mabaruma 64
Mabuiag Island 160
Macao City 90
Macapá 19
Macas 44
MacCarthy 56
Macedonia 182
Maceió 19
Macenta 63
Macerata 78
Machala 44
Machanao 61
Macina 94
Mackenzie 111
Mâcon 52
Macouba 97
Macouria 53
MacPherson 145
Macuata 49
Madang 124
Madaniyin 162
Madhya Pradesh 69
Madingou 35
Madison 174
Madras 70
Madre de Dios (Bolivia) 18
Madre de Dios (Peru) 18

Madrid 149
Madriz 115
Madsoua 115
Madug 146
Maebashi 80
Maehongson 158
Magadan 168
Magallanes 30
Magallanes y Antártica Chilena
  29
Maganoy 128
Magaria 115
Magdalena 34
Magdeburg 43
Magherafelt 173
Magnessia 58
Maguindanao 128
Magwe 22
Mahadhah 122
Mahakali 107
Maharashtra 69
Mahasarakham 157
Mahé 143
Mahmud-Ragi 1
Maia 4
Maiana 84
Maidstone 172
Maiduguri 117
Maikop 167
Maimana 1
Maine 174
Maine-et-Loir 52
Maine Soroa 116
Mainz 181
Maio 25
Majunga 91
Majuro (Madagascar) 95
Majuro (T.T.P.I.) 161
Makefu 117
Makeni 143
Maketeng 87
Makhachkala 167
Makin 84
Makira-Ulawa 146
Makoukou 55
Makung 32
Makurdi 116
Makwa 106
Malabo 46
Malacca 92
Malaeoloa 4

217

Marigot (Martinique) 97
Marin 96
Marinduque 127
Maripasoula 53
Maritîme 158
Marjoyoun 86
Markazi 71
Marlborough 110
Marne 52
Marne (Haute-) 52
Maroua 24
Maroun 74
Marowijne 152
Marrakech 103
Marri 123
Marseille 50
Marsh Harbour 9
Marshalls 161
Martinborough 113
Marton 113
Maryland (U.S.A.) 174
Maryland (Liberia) 88
Masaya 115
Masbate 127
Mascara 3
Maseru 87
Mashonaland North 184
Mashonaland South 184
Masindi 166
Massa 76
Massa-Carrara 76
Massachusetts 174
Massacre 42
Massana 5
Masterton (county) 110
Masterton (borough) 113
Mat 2
Mata Utu 180
Matabeleland North 184
Matabeleland South 184
Matadi 182
Matagulpa 115
Matale 150
Matam 142
Matamata (county) 110
Matamata (borough) 112
Matameye 116
Matanzas 38
Matara 150
Mataram 70
Mataura (French Polynesia) 54

Mataura (New Zealand) 114
Matera 77
Mati 128
Matina 38
Matlock 171
Matoury 53
Matrûh 45
Matsue 81
Matsuyama 81
Matthewtown 9
Matto Grosso 19
Matto Grosso do Sul 19
Mattu 47
Matulau 117
Maturin 178
Mau 49
Maughold 74
Mauke 36
Maun 18
Maunabo 132
Mauputasi 4
Mauren 89
May Pen 79
Mayaguana 9
Mayaguez 133
Mayahi 116
Maydan 1
Mayenne 52
Mayo 73
Mayo-Danaï 24
Mayo-Kebbi 27
Mayumba 55
Mazandaran 72
Mazar-i-Sharif 1
Mazaruni-Potaro 65
Mazatenango 62
Mbabane 153
M'Backe 142
M'Baiki 27
Mbale 166
Mbam 24
Mbandaka 183
Mbarara 166
Mbeya 156
Mbigou 55
M'Bomou 27
Mbouda 24
M'Bour 142
Mbuji-Mayi 183
Mchinji 91
Meath 73

Mecca 141
Mechi 106
Medan 70
Médéa 3
Medellín 34
Medinah 141
Médouneu 55
Méfou 24
Meghalya 69
Mehedinţi 136
Mejit 95
Mékambo 55
Mekele 47
Meknès 103
Melbourne 8
Melekeiok Municipality 11
Melilla 149
Melun 52
Menado 70
Mende 52
Méndez 17
Mendi 124
Mendoza 7
Meneng 106
Menongue 5
Ménoua 24
Menûfîya 45
Merca 146
Mérida 100
Mérida 178
Merizo 61
Mersch 89
Merseyside 171
Mersin 163
Meshed 71
Messenia 58
Messina 78
Meta 34
Metz 52
Meurthe-et-Moselle 52
Meuse 52
Mexicali 99
México 99
Mexico City 99
M'Foulenzem 55
Miaoli 32
Michael 74
Michigan 174
Michoachán 99
Micoud 139
Mid Glamorgan 172

Middle Caicos 164
Middle Island 138
Middlesborough 171
Middleburg 107
Middlegate 118
Midi-Pyrénées 50
Midlands 184
Midway islands 100
Mie 81
Miercurea Ciuc 136
Mifi 24
Mikhailovgrad 21
Mikkeli 50
Miladummudulu 93
Milan 76
Milano 77
Mili 95
Milne Bay 124
Milton 113
Mimongo 55
Minas Gerais 19
Mindefo 25
Mindoro Occidental 127
Mindoro Oriental 127
Minh Hai 179
Minna 117
Minnesota 174
Minsk 166
Minvoul 55
Minya 45
Miquelon 139
Miranda 178
Mirditë 2
Mirpur 123
Misaan 72
Misamis Occidental 127
Misamis Oriental 127
Misiones (Argentina) 7
Misiones (Paraguay) 125
Miskolc 67
Mississippi 174
Missolonghi 57
Missouri 174
Misurata 88
Mitiaro 36
Mito 80
Mitú 34
Mitylini 58
Mitzic 55
Miyagi 80
Miyazaki 81

Mizoram 69
Mizque 17
Mkokotoni 156
Mmabatho 147
Moa Island 160
Moabi 55
Moanda 55
Mobaye 27
Moca (Dominican Republic) 42
Moca (Puerto Rico) 134
Moçambique 104
Mocâmedes 5
Mochudi 18
Mocoa 34
Modena 77
Modesto Omiste 17
Moen (Micronesia) 100
Moen (T.T.P.I.) 161
Mogadishu 146
Mogilev 169
Mohale's Hoek 87
Mohamedia 103
Mohamand 123
Moindou 109
Moka 98
Mokhotlong 87
Mokolo 24
Mold 172
Moldavian S.S.R. 167
Moldo 121
Molepolole 18
Molise 76
Mon 22
Monaco-Ville 101
Monaghan 73
Monagas 178
Monaragalla 150
Mondal Kiri 83
Mong Kok 66
Mongo 27
Mongu 183
Mono 13
Monrovia 87
Mons 12
Mont-Dare 109
Mont-de-Marsan 51
Montana 174
Montauban 52
Monte Carlo 101
Montecristi 42
Montegiardino 140

Montego Bay 79
Monteria 34
Monterrey 99
Montes de Oca 37
Montes de Ora 38
Montevideo 176
Montgomery 173
Montpellier 50
Montserrado 88
Montsinérv-Tonnégrande 53
Mopti 93
Mopto 94
Moquegua 126
Mora 37
Morant Bay 79
Moravia (Costa Rica) 37
Morbihan 52
Mordovian 167
Møre og Romsdal 121
Morelia 99
Morelos 99
Morioka 80
Moriscal Estigarriba 125
Morne Rouge 96
Morne Vert 97
Morobe 124
Morogoro 156
Mörön 102
Morona-Santiago 44
Moroni 34
Moroto 166
Morovis 133
Morpeth 172
Morrinsville 112
Moscow 166
Moselle 52
Mosgiel 113
Moshi 156
Moss 120
Mostaganem 3
Motueka 113
Mouila 55
Moulins 51
Moulmein (Burma) 22
Moulmein (Singapore) 145
Moundou 27
Mt. Albert 111
Mt. Athos 57
Mt. Collinson 67
Mt. Eden 111
Mount Fortune 6

Obo   27
Obo-Zemio   27
Obock   41
Obwalden   154
O'Connor   17
Ocotepeque   66
Octotal   115
Oddur   146
Odense   41
Odessa   169
Odienné   79
Odongh Meanchey   83
Odongk   83
Offaly   73
Ofu   4
Ogooué-Ivindo   55
Ogooué-Lolo   55
Ogooué-Maritîme   55
Ogun   116
Ohakune   112
Ohinemuri   110
Ohio   174
Oio   64
Oise   52
Oita   81
Okahandja   105
Okakarara   105
Okayama   81
Okinawa   81
Oklahoma   174
Oklahoma City   174
Okondja   55
Ölafsfjördur   68
Olancho   66
Olei   120
Ölgiy   101
Olímpo   125
Olongapo   128
Olosega   4
Olstyn   131
Olsztyńskie   131
Olt   136
Olympia   174
Omagh   173
Omaruru   105
Omasuyos   16
Ombella-M'Poko   27
Omboué   55
Omega   105
Ömnögov   102
Omsk   168

Onchan   74
Ondangwa   105
Ondo   116
Öndörhaan   102
One Tree Hill   112
Onehunga   112
Ontoa   84
Ontario   25
Oost-Vlaanderen   12
Opole   131
Opolskie   131
Oporto   132
Opotiki   110
Oppland   121
Opuwo   105
Oradea   136
Orange Free State   147
Orange Walk   13
Oranjestad   108
Ordino   5
Ordu   163
Ordzhonikidze   167
Oreamundo   37
Örebro   153
Oregon   174
Orel   168
Orenburg   168
Orense   149
Orissa   69
Orkney   172
Orleans   50
Ormoc   129
Orne   52
Orocovis   133
Oropeza   16
Oroquieta   127
Orotina   37
Oroua   110
Oruro   16
Osa   38
Osaka   81
Osford   111
Osh   170
Oshakati   105
Oslo   120
Osorno   30
Östergötland   153
Osteroy   48
Ostersund   154
Østfold   120
Ostrava   40

Phuket 157
Phumi Samraong 83
Phunchholing 15
Phuthaditjhaba 147
Piacenza 77
Piako 110
Piatra Neamţ 136
Piauí 19
Picardie 50
Pichincha 44
Picton 113
Piemonte 76
Pieria 58
Pierre 174
Pietermaritzburg 147
Pila 131
Pilar 125
Pilskie 131
Pinar del Río 38
Pingtung 32
Piotrków Trybunalski 131
Piotrkowskie 131
Piraeus 58
Pisa 76
Pistoria 76
Pita 63
Piteşti 136
Piti 61
Piura 126
Plaines Wilhelms 98
Planken 89
Plateau 116
Plateaux 35
Plateaux de Nord-Mossi 175
Plevin 21
Plock 131
Plockie 131
Ploieşti 136
Plovdiv 21
Plymouth (Montserrat) 102
Plzeň 40
Poás 37
Pobé 13
Pococí 38
Podor 142
Pogradec 2
Pohangina 110
Pohjois-Karjala 49
Poindimié 108
Point Blackbourne 118
Point Hunter 118

Pointe Michael 42
Pointe-à-Pitre 60
Pointe Noire (Congo) 35
Pointe-Noire (Guadeloupe) 61
Poitiers 50
Poitou-Charentes 50
Pokhara 106
Polonnaruwa 150
Poltava 169
Polyghyros 58
Ponape (Micronesia) 100
Ponape (T.T.P.I.) 161
Ponce 133
Ponce I Municipality 133
Ponce II Municipality 133
Pondicherry 69
Ponérihouen 108
Ponta Delgado 132
Pontevedra 149
Pontianak 70
Pontoise 52
Pool 35
Poopó 17
Popayán 34
Popondetta 124
Pordenone 77
Porirua 113
Port Antonio 79
Port-au-Prince 65
Port-aux-Français 54
Port Blair 69
Port Chalmers 113
Port-de-Paix 65
Port Egmont 48
Port Gentil 55
Port Harcourt 116
Port Laoighis 73
Port-Louis (Guadeloupe) 61
Port-Louis (Mauritius) 98
Port Maria 79
Port Moresby 124
Port-of-Spain 161
Port Said 45
Port Sudan 151
Port-Vila 176
Portadown 173
Portalegre 132
Portland (Jamaica) 79
Pórto Alegre 19
Porto Amélia 104
Porto Novo (Cape Verde) 25

Porto-Novo (Benin)   13
Pôrto Velho   19
Portoviejo   44
Portsmouth   42
Portuguesa   178
Porvenir (Chile)   30
Posadas   7
Potenza   76
Potong Pasir   145
Potsdam   43
Potsí   16
Pouebo   108
Pouembout   108
Pouthisat   83
Powell   93
Powys   172
Poya   108
Poznań   131
Poznanskie   131
Prachinburi   157
Prachuapkirikhan   157
Prague (Praha)   40
Praia   25
Praslin   143
Preah Vihear   83
Precheur   97
Presidente Hayes   125
Preston   172
Pretoria   147
Preveza   58
Prey Veng   83
Prince Edward Island   25
Prince of Wales Island   160
Princess Town   161
Principe   141
Priština   182
Privas   51
Prosperidad   128
Provence-Côte d'Azur   50
Providence   174
Providenciales   164
Przemyskie   131
Przemyśl   131
Pskov   168
Puebla   100
Puerto Ayacucho   178
Puerto Baquerizo   45
Puerto Barrios   62
Puerto Carreño   34
Puerto Montt   29
Puerto Natales   30

Puerto Plata   42
Puerto Princesa   127
Puerto Princessa Chartered City
   129
Puerto Williams   30
Puglia   76
Pukapuka   36
Pukë   2
Pukekohe   112
Pulu Anna Island   12
Punakha   15
Punata   17
Punch   123
Punggol   144
Punjab   70
Punjab (Pakistan)   123
Puno   126
Punta Arenas   29
Punta Gorda   13
Puntarenas   36
Puriscal   36
Pusan   148
Putaruru   112
Puttalam   150
Putuakhali   10
Putumayo   34
Puy-de-Dôme   52
Puyo   44
Pyongan-Pukto   119
Pyongan-Namdo   119
Pyongyang   118
Pyrénées (Hautes-)   52
Pyrénées-Atlantiques   52
Pyrénées-Orientales   52
Pyrgos   58

Qabis   162
Qacha's Nek   87
Qadisiya   72
Qafsah   162
Qal cat Bishah   141
Qala-i-Naw   1
Qalyûbîya   45
Qandahar   1
Qassim   141
Qena   45
Qinghai   31
Qisan   141
Quanary   53
Quang Nam-Da-Nang   179
Quang Ninh   179

Quebec 25
Quebec City 25
Quebradillas 134
Queensland (Australia) 8
Queenstown (New Zealand) 114
Queenstown (Singapore) 144
Quelimane 104
Quémé 13
Querétaro 100
Quetta 123
Quezaltenango 62
Quezon 127
Quezon Chartered City 129
Qui Nhon 179
Quibdó 34
Quiche 62
Quijarro 17
Quillacollo 17
Quillota 30
Quimper 51
Quindío 34
Quineitra 75
Quintana Roo 100
Quirino 127
Quito 44
Qurayyat 141
Quriyat 122
Quthing 87
Qwaqwa 147

Ra 49
Rabat 103
Rabat-Salé 103
Rabaul 124
Rach Gia 179
Rachaíya 86
Radin Mas 145
Radnor 14
Radom 131
Raetihi 112
Rafah 75
Ragged Island 9
Raglan 109
Ragusa 78
Rajasthan 70
Rajbiraj 106
Rajshani 10
Rakahanga 36
Rakai 166
Rakiraki 49
Raleigh 174

Ramaadi 72
Ramla 75
Ramomskie 131
Ramotswa 18
Rancagua 29
Rangamati 10
Rangárvallasýsla 68
Rangiora 111
Rangiroa 54
Rangitikei 110
Rangoon 22
Rangpur 10
Ranong 157
Ranyah 141
Rapati 107
Rarotonga 36
Ras al Khaimah 170
Rasht 71
Ratanakiri 83
Ratburi 156
Ratnapura 150
Ravaniemi 49
Ravenna 77
Rawson 7
Rayong 157
Razgrad 21
Reading 171
Recife 19
Red Sea 45
Rédange 90
Reggio di Calabria 77
Reggio nell'Emilia 77
Regina (Canada) 25
Régina (French Guiana) 53
Rehoboth 105
Rehovat 75
Reims 50
Remich 90
Remire-Montjoly 53
Rennes 50
Réo 175
Resita 136
Resistencia 7
Retalhuleu 62
Rethymnon 58
Rewa 49
Reykjavik 68
Rezayeh 71
Rhin (Bas-) 52
Rhin (Haut-) 52
Rhineland Palatinate 181

Rhode Island 174
Rhodes 58
Rhône 52
Rhône-Alpes 50
Riau 70
Ribe 41
Ribeira Grande 25
Riccarton 113
Richmond (U.S.A.) 174
Richmond (New Zealand) 113
Rieti 77
Riffa 9
Rift Valley 84
Riga 167
Rîmnicu Vîlcea 136
Rincon 134
Ringkøbing 41
Rio Branco 19
Rio Claro 161
Rio de Janeiro 19
Rio Gallegos 7
Rio Grande 133
Rio Grande do Norte 19
Rio Grande do Sul 19
Rio Muni 47
Rió Negro (Argentina) 7
Río Negro (Uruguay) 176
Rio San Juan 115
Riobamba 44
Riohacha 34
Risaralda 34
Rivas 115
River Valley 144
Rivera 176
Rivers 116
Riverton 114
Rivière-du-Rempart 98
Rivière Pilote 96
Rivière Salée 96
Riyadh 141
Rizal 127
Rize 164
Roadtown 20
Roatán 66
Robert 96
Robertsport 88
Rocadas 5
Rocha 176
Rochore 144
Rock Sound 9
Rocky Point 118

Rodez 51
Rodney 109
Rodopi 58
Rogaland 121
Roi-et 157
Roma 77
Romblon 127
Rome 76
Ronawi 106
Rondônia 19
Rongelap 96
Rønne 41
Roraima 19
Rosalie 42
Roscommon 73
Rose Belle 98
Roseau 42
Roskilde 41
Rosso 97
Rostock 43
Rostov 168
Rostov-On-Don 168
Rota 120
Rotorua (county) 110
Rotorua (city) 112
Rouen 50
Rouen 52
Roura 53
Rovigo 76
Rovno 169
Roxas 127
Roxas Chartered City 129
Roxburgh 114
Rrëshen 2
Rufisque 142
Ruggell 89
Rukungiri 166
Rukwa 156
Rumbek 151
Rumphi 91
Runanga 113
Rundu 105
Rupununi 65
Rushen 74
Russe 21
Russian S.F.S.R. 167
Rustaq 121
Ruvuma 156
Ruyigi 23
Ryazan 168
Rzeszów 131

St. Ouen 29
St. Patrick (Dominica) 42
St. Patrick (Grenada) 60
St. Patrick (St. Vincent) 140
St. Patrick (Trinidad) 161
St. Paul (U.S.A.) 174
St. Paul (Antigua) 6
St. Paul (Dominica) 42
St. Paul (Nevis) 138
Saint-Paul (Réunion) 135
St. Paul (St. Kitts) 138
St. Paul's (St. Helena) 137
St. Peter (Antigua) 6
St. Peter (Barbados) 11
St. Peter (Dominica) 42
St. Peter-in-the-Wood 28
St. Peter (Jersey) 29
St. Peter (Montserrat) 102
St. Peter Port 28
St. Peter (St. Kitts) 138
St. Phillip (Antigua) 6
St. Phillip (Barbados) 11
Saint-Philippe (Réunion) 135
St. Pierre 139
Saint-Pierre (Martinique) 96
St. Sampson 28
St. Saviour (Guernsey) 28
St. Saviour (Jersey) 29
St. Thomas and St. John 175
St. Thomas (Barbados) 11
St. Thomas (Jamaica) 79
St. Thomas (Nevis) 138
St. Thomas (St. Kitts) 138
Sainte-Anne (Guadeloupe) 61
Sainte-Anne (Martinique) 97
Sainte-Denis 135
Sanite-Luce 96
Sainte-Marie (Martinique) 96
Sainte-Marie (Réunion) 135
Sainte-Rose (Guadeloupe) 61
Sainte-Rose (Réunion) 135
Sainte-Suzanne (Réunion) 135
Saipan 120
Saipan (T.T.P.I.) 161
Saitama 80
Sajama 17
Sakarya 164
Sakété 13
Sakhalin 168
Sakonnakhorn 157
Sal 25

Sal-Rei 25
Salaah Eddeen 72
Sălaj 136
Salalah 121
Salamá 62
Salamanca 149
Salamat 27
Salazar 5
Salazie 135
Salcedo 43
Salekhard 167
Salem 174
Salerno 77
Salgótarján 67
Salima 91
Salinas 133
Sallyan 107
Salomon 20
Salt Cay 164
Salt Cay Town 164
Salt Lake City 174
Salta 7
Saltillo 99
Salto 176
Salvador 19
Salzburg 8
Sam Neua 85
Samaná 43
Samangan 1
Samarinda 70
Samarkand 170
Samos 58
Samsun 164
Samutjsrakan 157
Samutsakhorn 157
Samutsongkhram 157
San 94
San Andés 34
San Andés y Providencia 34
San Antonio (Chile) 30
San Antonio (Marianas) 120
San Blas 123
San Carlos (Costa Rica) 37
San Carlos (Nicaragua) 115
San Carlos (Negros Occidental,
    Philippines) 129
San Carlos (Pangasinan,
    Philippines) 128
San Carlos (Venezuela) 178
San Cristôbal (Dominican Repub-
    lic) 43
San Cristôbal (Venezuela) 178

Sétif 3
Settat 103
Setúbal 132
Severočeský 40
Severomoravský 40
Sevilla 150
Sèvres (Deux-) 52
Seydhisfjördur 69
s'Gravenhage 107
Sha Tin 66
Shaanxi 31
Shaba 183
Shabellaha Dhexe 146
Shabellaha Hoose 146
Shabwah 148
Shah Alam 92
Shahrekord 71
Sham Shui Po 66
Shan 22
Shandong 31
Shanghai 31
Shanxi 31
Sharjah 170
Sharm Esh-Sheikh 75
Sharon 75
Sharqîya 45
Shek Wu Hui 66
Shell Beach 28
Shenyang 31
Shepherd 177
s'Hertogenbosch 107
Shetland 172
Shibarkhan 1
Shibin-el-Kôm 45
Shiga 81
Shillong 69
Shimane 81
Shinas 122
Shingbe 15
Shinyanga 156
Shiraz 71
Shiselweni 153
Shizuoka 81
Shkodër 2
Shoa 47
Shrewsbury 172
Shropshire 172
Shumen 21
Sibiti 35
Sibiu 136
Sichuan 31

Sicilia 76
Sidamo 47
Sidi-Bel-Abbès 3
Sidi Bu Zayd 162
Siedlce 131
Siedleckie 131
Siem Reap 83
Siena 76
Sieradz 131
Sieradzkie 131
Sigatoka 49
Siglap 144
Siglufjördhur 69
Siguiri 63
Siirt 164
Sikasso 93
Sikkim 70
Silay 129
Silhouette 143
Silistra 21
Silvassa 69
Silyanah 162
Simaawa 72
Simbu 124
Simferopol 169
Simla 70
Sinai 45
Sinaiana 61
Sinaloa 100
Sincelejo 34
Sind 123
Sindara 55
Sine-Saloum 142
Singapore City 144
Singave 180
Singhburi 157
Singida 156
Sinnamary 53
Sinoe 88
Sinola 184
Sinop 164
Sinuiji 119
Sion 154
Siparia 161
Siquijor 127
Siquirres 38
Siracusa 78
Sithandone 86
Sitrah 9
Sivas 164
Siyabuswa 147

Stara Zagora 22
Stavanger 121
Steinkjor 121
Stepanokert 168
Stephen Island 166
Stewart Island 111
Stirling 172
Stockholm 153
Stonoway 172
Storstøms 41
Strabane 173
Strandasýsla 68
Strasbourg 50
Stratford 110
Strathallon 111
Strathclyde 172
Středočeský 40
Středoslovenský 40
Stromoy 48
Stung Treng 83
Stuttgart 181
Stykkisholmur 68
Sua 4
Suceava 136
Suchitepéquez 62
Sucre (Colombia) 34
Sucre (Venezuela) 178
Sud Chichas 17
Sud Cinti 16
Sud (Haiti) 65
Sud Est (Haiti) 65
Sud Lípez 17
Sud (New Caledonia) 109
Sud-Ouest (Cameroon) 23
Sud Yungas 16
Suddie 64
Suderoy Nodre 48
Suderoy Sondre 48
Sudhur-Múlasýsla 68
Sudhur-Thingeyjarsýsla 68
Suez 45
Suffolk 172
Sühbaatar 102
Suhl 43
Sukho-thai 158
Sukhumi 167
Sukkertoppen 59
Sulawesi Selatan 70
Sulawesi Tengah 70
Sulawesi Tenggara 70
Sulaimaniya 72

Sulawesi Utara 70
Sultan Kudarat 128
Sulu 128
Sumail 122
Sumatera Berat 70
Sumatera Selatan 70
Sumatera Utara 70
Sumay 61
Sumba 48
Sumy 169
Sunyani 56
Suphanburi 157
Sur 122
Surabaya 70
Suratthani 157
Surigao 127
Surigao del Norte 127
Surigao del Sur 127
Surin 157
Suriname 152
Surkhan-Darya 170
Surrey 172
Susah 162
Susupe 120
Suvadiva 93
Suwaiq 122
Suwalskie 131
Suwarrow 36
Suwon 148
Svay Rieng 83
Sverdlovsk 168
Swain's Island 4
Swakopmund 105
Swansea 172
Swat 123
Sydney 8
Syktyvkar 167
Sylhet 10
Syr-Darya 170
Szabolcs-Szatmár 67
Szezecin 131
Szezecinskie 131
Szeged 67
Székesfehérvár 67
Szekszárd 67
Szolnok 67
Szombathely 67

Tabasco 100
Tabiteuea 84
Tabligbo 158

Wairoa (county) 110
Wairoa (borough) 112
Waitake 111
Waitara 112
Waitemata 111
Waitomo 114
Waiuku 112
Waitotara 110
Wakayama 81
Wake Islet 180
Walbrzych 131
Walbrzyskie 131
Wallace 111
Walvis Bay (Namibia) 105
Walvis Bay (South Africa) 147
Wan Chai 66
Wanganui (county) 110
Wanganui (borough) 112
Wangdu Phrodang 15
Warnes 17
Warraber Island 160
Warsaw 130
Warszawskie 130
Warwick 172
Warwick (Bermuda) 15
Warwickshire 172
Washington, D.C. 173
Washington (Kiribati) 84
Washington (U.S.A.) 174
Waterford 73
Waverley 114
Wāw 151
Wé 109
Webag 124
Weipa Island 160
Wejh 141
Wellington 109
Wellington Borough 113
West Azerbaijan 71
West Bay 26
West Bengal 70
West Berbice 64
West Berlin 180
West Coast (Singapore) 145
West Demerara 64
West End 26
West End Village 6
West Falkland 48
West Glamorgan 172
West Greenland 59
West Island (Cocos) 33

West Lake (Tanzania) 156
West Midlands 171
West New Britain 124
West Sepik 124
West Sussex 172
West Virginia 174
West-Vlaanderen 12
West Yorkshire 171
Western Australia 8
Western (Bahrain) 9
Western (Fiji) 49
Western (Gambia) 56
Western (Ghana) 56
Western Highlands 124
Western Isles (Scotland) 172
Western (Kenya) 84
Western (Malta) 95
Western Mindanao 128
Western (Papua New Guinea)
   124
Western Samar 127
Western (Sierra Leone) 143
Western (Solomons) 146
Western (Torres Straight) 160
Western Tutuila 4
Western Visayas 128
Western (Zambia) 183
Westland 110
Westmeath 73
Westmoreland (Jamaica) 79
Westport 113
Wete 156
Wewak 124
Wexford 73
Whagarei 111
Whakatane 114
Whampoa 145
Whangarei 109
Whangaroa 109
Whitehorse 25
Wicklow 73
Wien 8
Wiesbaden 181
Willemstad 108
Wiltshire 172
Wiltz 90
Winchester (U.K.) 171
Windhoek 104
Windward (Montserrat) 102
Windward (St. Kitts-Nevis) 138
Windward Islands 108